A DOLL'S HOUSE

BY
HENRIK IBSEN

ADAPTED BY
FRANK McGUINNESS

DPS
Classics

SPECIAL NOTE

Anyone receiving permission to produce A DOLL'S HOUSE is required to give credit to the Author as sole and exclusive Author of the Play on the title page of all programs distributed in connection with performances of the Play and in all instances in which the title of the Play appears, including printed or digital materials for advertising, publicizing or otherwise exploiting the Play and/or a production thereof. The name of the Author must appear on a separate line, in which no other name appears, immediately beneath the title and in size of type equal to 50% of the size of the largest, most prominent letter used for the title of the Play. No person, firm or entity may receive credit larger or more prominent than that accorded the Author. The following acknowledgments must appear on the title page of all programs distributed in connection with performances of the Play:

A DOLL'S HOUSE was previously produced at
the Playhouse Theatre in London by Thelma Holt.

Produced on Broadway by Bill Kenwright in association with Thelma Holt.

SPECIAL NOTE ON SONGS AND RECORDINGS

Dramatists Play Service, Inc. neither holds the rights to nor grants permission to use any songs or recordings mentioned in the Play. Permission for performances of copyrighted songs, arrangements or recordings mentioned in this Play is not included in our license agreement. The permission of the copyright owner(s) must be obtained for any such use. For any songs and/or recordings mentioned in the Play, other songs, arrangements, or recordings may be substituted provided permission from the copyright owner(s) of such songs, arrangements or recordings is obtained; or songs, arrangements or recordings in the public domain may be substituted.

PREFACE

In 1871, eight years before he wrote *A Doll's House*, Ibsen met a Norwegian girl called Laura Petersen. Ibsen took quite a fancy to her, and called her his 'skylark.'

In 1872 she married a Danish schoolmaster, Victor Kieler, who subsequently contracted tuberculosis. His doctors prescribed a warmer climate, but they were poor, and Victor became hysterical at the mention of money. Laura arranged a loan without her husband's knowledge, for which a friend stood security. The trip to Italy thus financed was successful, and Victor made a good recovery.

Two years later, however, repayment of the loan was demanded. Laura did not have the money herself, dared not tell her husband and, worse, still, the friend who had stood security had himself fallen on hard times. Laura attempted to pay off the loan by forging a check. The forgery was discovered, the bank refused payment, and Laura was forced to tell the whole story to her husband.

Despite the fact that she had done it purely to save his life, Victor Kieler treated Laura like a criminal. He claimed that she was an unfit wife and mother and, when she suffered a nervous breakdown, he had her committed to a public asylum, and demanded a separation so that the children could be removed from Laura's care. She was discharged after a month, and managed to persuade Victor to take her back for the children's sake, which he eventually, but grudgingly, agreed to do.

In September 1878, only a couple months after hearing about Laura's committal to the asylum, Ibsen began work on *A Doll's House*. In his notes he wrote the following: A woman cannot be herself in modern society, with laws made by men and with prosecutors and judges who assess female conduct from a male standpoint.

Frank McGuinness' adaptation of Ibsen's A DOLL'S HOUSE was produced on Broadway by Bill Kenwright in association with Thelma Holt Productions, at the Belasco Theatre, on April 2, 1997. The creative team was as in its original production in London. The general management on Broadway was by Stuart Thompson Productions; the production supervisor was Gene O'Donovan; and the production stage manager was Tom Santopietro. The cast was as follows:

NORA HELMER . . . . Janet McTeer
TORVALD HELMER . . . . Owen Teale
KRISTINE LINDE . . . . Jan Maxwell
NILS KROGSTAD . . . . Peter Gowan
DR. RANK . . . . John Carlisle
ANNE-MARIE (THE NANNY) . . . . Robin Howard
HELENE (THE MAID) . . . . Rose Stockton
THE MESSENGER . . . . John Ottavino
BOBBY AND IVAN (THE HELMER'S CHILDREN) . . . . Liam Aiken
and Paul Tiesler

Frank McGuinness' adaptation of Ibsen's A DOLL'S HOUSE received its premiere at the Playhouse Theatre at London's West End, in London, England, on October 24, 1996. It was produced by Thelma Holt Productions. It was directed by Anthony Page; the set and costume designs were by Diedre Clancy; the lighting design was by Peter Mumford; the sound design was by Scott Myers and John Owens. The music was composed by Jason Carr; and the choreography was by Caroline Pope. The cast was as follows:

NORA HELMER . . . . Janet McTeer
TORVALD HELMER . . . . Owen Teale
KRISTINE LINDE . . . . Gabrielle Lloyd
NILS KROGSTAD . . . . Peter Gowan
DR. RANK . . . . John Carlisle
ANNE-MARIE (THE NANNY) . . . . Illona Linthwaite
HELENE (THE MAID) . . . . Judith Hepburn
THE MESSENGER . . . . Murray McArthur
BOBBY AND IVAN (THE HELMER'S CHILDREN) . . . . . Luke Atherton,
James Atherton, Gregory Hall,
Charles Wyn-Davies

SCENE

The Helmers' Living Room
A small Norwegian town. 1879

ACT ONE
Christmas Eve. Morning.

ACT TWO
Christmas Day. Late Afternoon.

ACT THREE
The Day After Christmas. Night.

To Sheila Lemon
with love

A DOLL'S HOUSE

ACT ONE

A warm, well-furnished room, reflecting more taste than expense. At stage right, a door leads to a hall. Another door, stage left, leads to Helmer's study. There is a piano between these two doors. There is a door in the middle of the wall, stage left, and a window further downstage. There is a round table near the window, with armchairs and a small sofa. Somewhat towards the back in the side wall stage right, there is a door, and further downstage on the same wall a stove covered in white tiles with a couple of armchairs and a rocking chair in front of it. Between the stove and the side door there is a small table. There are engravings on the walls. There is a what-not with china pieces and other little knick-knacks on it. There is a small bookcase with expensively bound books in it. The floor is carpeted, and there is a fire burning in the stove. It is a winter's day.

A bell rings in the hall and we hear the door open shortly afterwards. Nora enters the room, humming cheerfully to herself.

She wears outdoor clothes and carries a number of packages. She puts them on the table stage right. She has left open the door to the hall and we can see a messenger carrying a Christmas tree. He has given a basket to the Maid, Helene, who opened the door to them.

NORA: The Christmas tree, hide it away safely, Helene. Until this evening. Don't let the children see it until it's been decorated. *(She takes out her purse.)* How much —
MESSENGER: A fifty ore.
NORA: A hundred, take it. Keep the change. Merry Christmas.

7

MESSENGER: Merry Christmas. *(The messenger thanks her and leaves. Nora closes the door. She keeps laughing, quietly, cheerfully, as she takes her coat off. She takes out a bag of macaroons from her pocket and eats a few. She then walks cautiously towards her husband's door and listens.)*

NORA: Yes, he is at home. *(Nora hums again as she goes to the table stage R. Helmer calls from his study.)*

HELMER: Is that skylark chirping out there, is that who's out there? *(Nora is busily opening some of the parcels.)*

NORA: Yes, yes.

HELMER: Squirrel, squirrel is that who's out there?

NORA: Yes, yes.

HELMER: When did squirrel scamper home?

NORA: Just now. *(She puts the bag of macaroons in her pocket and wipes her mouth.)* Torvald come and see what I've bought.

HELMER: I can't be disturbed. *(After a while he opens the door, looks out, pen in hand.)* Did you say bought? All of this? I've a little bird who likes to fritter money, has that little bird been frittering again?

NORA: But darling, we can spend a little more can't we?

HELMER: You know very well we can't spend a fortune.

NORA: I didn't say that, did I. I just said a little bit. Anyway you're going to get a big salary and you will earn pots and pots of money.

HELMER: After New Year yes, but it will be a full three-months before the salary is due.

NORA: So what? We can borrow till then.

HELMER: Nora! *(He goes and playfully pinches her ear.)* Are you being a silly girl? Say I borrowed a thousand and you let it slip through your fingers during Christmas, and then a tile falls off the roof, hits me on the head, and flattens me. *(Nora puts her hand over his mouth.)*

NORA: Don't. Don't say such horrible things.

HELMER: What if something horrible happened, Nora?

NORA: If something that horrible did happen, I wouldn't care if we had debts or not.

HELMER: The people I've borrowed from would care.

NORA: Them? They're strangers. Who cares about strangers?

HELMER: Now, be serious, Nora. You know what I think. Look, the two of us have managed well enough up to now. We still have to manage for a short while, and we will, because we must. *(Nora goes towards the stove. He follows her.)* Who's hanging her head, is it my little skylark? She mustn't. *(He takes out his wallet.)* Nora, look, what have I here? *(Nora turns briskly.)*

NORA: Money!

HELMER: Yes. *(He hands her some notes.)* I know how much money needs to be spent in a house at Christmas. *(Nora counts.)*

NORA: Ten — twenty — thirty — forty. Torvald, thank you. I will stretch it out, I promise.

HELMER: Yes, do that. You must do that.

NORA: I will, I promise. Now please let me show you what I've bought. For virtually nothing. New clothes, here for Ivan — and a sword. A horse for Bobby, and here, a trumpet. A doll and a cradle for Emmy. Nothing much! She'll soon rip it to ribbons anyway. I got some material for the maids — make dresses and scarves. Old Anne-Marie should get something better really.

HELMER: What lurks in that particular parcel? *(Nora screams.)*

NORA: No, Torvald, you're not to see that until this evening.

HELMER: I see. What have you dreamt up for yourself? Well, tell me, you little spendthrift?

NORA: For me? I don't want anything.

HELMER: You most certainly do. Tell me what you'd like — something sensible.

NORA: I don't know. Yes, I do. Torvald, listen to me.

HELMER: What? *(Without looking at him, Nora fingers his buttons.)*

NORA: If you could give me something, could you — could you —

HELMER: Say it, say it.

NORA: Money. Give me money, Torvald. As much as you think you can spare. I can buy something with it one of these days.

HELMER: No, Nora, really —

NORA: Oh darling, please. I've asked you ever so prettily. I know what, I could hang it on the Christmas tree, wrapped in beautiful gold paper. That would be fun, wouldn't it?

HELMER: What do we call little birds that like to fritter money.

NORA: Little fritter birds, yes, I know them well. Let's do as I say,

Torvald. I'll take time to think what I need most. That would be sensible, yes? *(He smiles.)*

HELMER: Sensible, yes. If you could only hold on to my money and buy something you really need. But it goes on the house and so many useless odds and ends and then I've to put my hand into my wallet all over again.

NORA: But Torvald —

HELMER: But nothing, my lovely, little Nora. *(He puts his arms around her waist.)* My little bird that fritters is so very sweet, but she does waste an awful lot of money.

NORA: How can you say that? I do try to save up all that I can. *(Helmer laughs.)*

HELMER: You do, you do. All that you can. But you can't. *(Nora turns and smiles, quietly pleased.)*

NORA: Honestly, Torvald, if you only knew how many expenses singing birds and squirrels have.

HELMER: You're a fascinating little creature. So like your father. You try every trick to get at money. When you do get it, it slips through your fingers. You never know how you spent it. Well, I have to take you as you are.

NORA: I wish I were more like my Papa.

HELMER: But I wouldn't want you any other way. Stay as you are, my lovely little singing bird. But you, Nora, you look quite — quite — devious today —

NORA: I do?

HELMER: You do, yes. Look into my eyes. *(Nora looks at him.)*

NORA: What? *(He wags his finger.)*

HELMER: Was a sweet tooth indulged in town today by any chance?

NORA: No.

HELMER: Did a sweet tooth stroll into a pastry shop?

NORA: No, honestly, Torvald —

HELMER: Helped itself to a macaroon or two?

NORA: No, honestly.

HELMER: All right! You know, I'm only joking — *(Nora goes to the table stage R.)*

NORA: Honestly, darling, I wouldn't do anything you didn't want me to.

HELMER: You've given me your word. So, my dearest Nora, keep your little festive secrets all to yourself. All will be revealed when the Christmas tree is lit. I have ordered wonderful wines. Nora, you can't imagine how much I'm looking forward to this evening.

NORA: Me too, and the children.

HELMER: It is so good to know that one has a secure, respectable position. And an ample salary. Isn't that so? It is a great pleasure to know that, yes?

NORA: Yes, it is wonderful!

HELMER: The hard times have all gone.

NORA: I know. Darling, I want to tell you how I think we can arrange things. Once Christmas is over — *(A bell rings in the hallway.)*

HELMER: I'm not at home. Remember that.

NORA: It's Dr. Rank. *(The Maid stands in the hall doorway.)*

MAID: Mrs. Helmer, there is a lady here to see you — a stranger.

NORA: Show her in. *(Helmer enters the study. The Maid shows Mrs. Linde into the room and closes the door behind her. Mrs. Linde is dressed in travelling clothes. She speaks timidly and a little reluctantly.)*

MRS. LINDE: Nora, hello. *(Nora is uncertain.)*

NORA: Hello —

MRS. LINDE: Oh, you don't recognize me.

NORA: No, I'm afraid I — *(She cries out.)* Wait a minute . . . Kristine! I don't believe you.

MRS. LINDE: Yes, it is me.

NORA: Kristine! I did not recognize you. I didn't. How could I — *(She speaks more quietly.)* Kristine, you've changed so much.

MRS. LINDE: I believe I have, yes. Nine, ten years, long years.

NORA: Is it that long since we last saw each other? It is, so it is. Did you make that long journey in winter? How brave of you.

MRS. LINDE: I arrived on the steamer this morning.

NORA: Oh for Christmas, of course, to have a good time. How lovely. We will have such fun. Oh my word, you're freezing. *(Nora helps her.)* Now, sit down by the warm stove. Shall I take your coat? No, you take the comfy chair. I'll take the rocking chair. That's better, now you look more like you used to look. It was just at first — you do look paler, Kristine, and perhaps a little thinner.

MRS. LINDE: And older, Nora, much older.

NORA: A little older, yes, perhaps, a tiny little bit. Not much, not much. *(She stops suddenly and looks serious.)* Oh, Kristine, I'm so sorry. Forgive me.

MRS. LINDE: Forgive you? Why, Nora?

NORA: You lost your husband.

MRS. LINDE: Three years ago, yes.

NORA: I read it in the newspapers. Kristine, do believe me, I meant so often to write to you then, but I just kept putting it off and things kept getting in the way.

MRS. LINDE: My dear Nora, I understand perfectly.

NORA: No, it was very bad of me. Didn't he leave you anything to live on?

MRS. LINDE: Nothing.

NORA: And no children?

MRS. LINDE: None.

NORA: Nothing at all then?

MRS. LINDE: He left me nothing, not even an ounce of grief.

NORA: Kristine, that's not possible. *(Mrs. Linde smiles sadly and strokes Nora's hair.)*

MRS. LINDE: These things do happen sometimes, Nora.

NORA: All on your own then. All on your own. That's awful. I have three such lovely children. Oh I didn't mean it like that. You can't see them just yet. The Nanny's taken them out. But tell me everything —

MRS. LINDE: No, no, no, you talk to me.

NORA: No, you start. I am not going to be selfish today. Today I will think only about you. Oh, I do have to tell you one thing. Have you heard our wonderful news?

MRS. LINDE: No, what?

NORA: My husband has just been made the new manager of the Joint Stock Bank.

MRS. LINDE: Your husband — that is wonderful —

NORA: Yes, I know. Being a lawyer is such an insecure profession. Oh I can't tell you how happy we are. When he starts work at the bank in the New Year he gets a huge salary and a fair share of bonuses. From then on we can live quite differently. We can do as we like. Oh Kristine, it is gorgeous to have pots and pots of money. Isn't it?

MRS. LINDE: Yes indeed, it must be lovely to have the basics.

NORA: No, more than the basics, pots and pots and pots of money. *(Mrs. Linde smiles.)*

MRS. LINDE: Nora, Nora, haven't you got any sense yet? Even in school you spent money like water.

NORA: I know, and Torvald says I still do but our life together hasn't been that easy. We've had very little money. We have both had to work hard.

MRS. LINDE: You as well?

NORA: Oh yes. Bits and pieces. Needlework, crocheting, embroidery — that sort of thing. Other things as well. The thing is, when we first got married obviously Torvald had to earn more money than before but in that first year he took on so much extra work he just couldn't take it and he became ill. Terribly, terribly ill and the doctors said it was absolutely necessary that we travelled south.

MRS. LINDE: Oh yes, you spent an entire year in Italy, didn't you?

NORA: We did. And it saved his life, Torvald's life. It was a wonderful year but it cost an awful lot of money.

MRS. LINDE: I would imagine so.

NORA: Four thousand, eight hundred kroner — a lot — a lot of money.

MRS. LINDE: You were very lucky that you had it.

NORA: Well, we had it from Papa, you know.

MRS. LINDE: I see. It was around the time your father died.

NORA: Yes, that's right. Can you believe it — I couldn't go to nurse him. I was stuck here, I was expecting Ivar to be born any day and I had Torvald to look after, and he was so ill, so ill. Do you remember my Papa? He was so dear to me, so kind — I never saw him again. That's the worst thing that's happened to me since I got married.

MRS. LINDE: I remember how fond you were of him. So then you left for Italy?

NORA: Yes, we left a month later.

MRS. LINDE: And your husband came back in good health?

NORA: Fit as a fiddle.

MRS. LINDE: But — the doctor?

NORA: I'm sorry?

MRS. LINDE: The gentleman who arrived at the same time as me? I thought the maid said....

NORA: Oh, Dr. Rank, yes. Oh no, this isn't a professional visit. He's Torvald's best friend. He drops by at least once a day. No, Torvald has not been ill for one moment since then. And the children are well, they're very healthy, and I am too. Oh Kristine! It is so wonderful to be alive and to be happy. Oh, that was so thoughtless of me — listen to me rabbiting on about myself. I'm so sorry. Don't be cross with me, don't. Would you tell me something? You know you said you didn't love your husband, why did you marry him? Tell me.

MRS. LINDE: My mother was alive then. She was bedridden. Helpless. I had two younger brothers. I had to take care of them. I could not refuse his offer. It wouldn't have been justifiable.

NORA: No, I don't suppose it would have, really. So he was rich, then?

MRS. LINDE: He did have money, but the whole business was shaky. Then he died, and everything collapsed. There was nothing left.

NORA: What happened?

MRS. LINDE: I managed a little shop. And then a little school. And anything else I could think of. These last three years, Nora, I haven't stopped working. That's over now, Nora. My poor mother's died, she doesn't need me. The boys don't either. They've found positions, they can look after themselves.

NORA: You must feel so relieved —

MRS. LINDE: No, empty. I cannot tell you how empty. Nothing to live for any more. *(She gets up uneasily.)* That's why I couldn't stay there any more. It must be easier to find work here. Something to keep me busy, to take my mind off things. I thought perhaps a job, some office job.

NORA: Kristine, no, it will wear you out and you look so exhausted already. Why don't you go for a holiday — *(Mrs. Linde goes to the window.)*

14

MRS. LINDE: Nora, I don't have a Papa to give me the money for the journey.

NORA: Don't be cross with me, don't. *(Mrs. Linde goes to her.)*

MRS. LINDE: I'm sorry, I've just become so bitter. I have to think about myself all the time. Do you know? When you told me of your good news I was happy not for you, but for myself.

NORA: What do you mean? Oh I see, you think Torvald might be able to help you?

MRS. LINDE: Yes, I do think that.

NORA: Well, he will, Kristine. Leave it to me. I'll ask him. I'll think of something he really likes. And I would really like to be able to help you.

MRS. LINDE: Nora, it's so kind of you, to help me — especially when you know so little of how difficult life can be —

NORA: Sorry?

MRS. LINDE: Dear God, you do some needlework, you embroider — you are a child, Nora.

NORA: Don't say that to me, don't talk down to me.

MRS. LINDE: I'm sorry.

NORA: You're as bad as the rest of them. You all think that I'm useless. Do you honestly think that I don't know how hard life can be —

MRS. LINDE: Nora dear, you've just told me about your troubles.

NORA: That was nothing. There's a big thing I've not told you.

MRS. LINDE: What do you mean?

NORA: You're proud that you worked so long and hard for your family, aren't you?

MRS. LINDE: Yes, I am.

NORA: Listen to me, Kristine. I've done something to be proud and happy about. I have.

MRS. LINDE: I don't doubt it. What is it?

NORA: Torvald must not hear this. He must never hear this. No one must know, Kristine. No one but you.

MRS. LINDE: What?

NORA: It was me who saved Torvald's life. I saved his life.

MRS. LINDE: You saved his life? How did you save it?

NORA: You know the trip to Italy I told you about — Torvald would be dead if he hadn't gone there —

MRS. LINDE: Yes, your father gave you the money you needed —

NORA: That's what Torvald thinks — that's what everyone thinks — but —

MRS. LINDE: But —

NORA: Not one penny from Papa. I found the money. I did.

MRS. LINDE: You, so much money —

NORA: Four thousand, eight hundred kroner — what do you say to that?

MRS. LINDE: So where did you get it from? You couldn't have borrowed it.

NORA: Why not?

MRS. LINDE: A wife is not allowed to borrow without her husband's consent, a wife —

NORA: What if the wife knows something about business? What if the wife knows how to use her brains, then —

MRS. LINDE: No, I do not understand —

NORA: Did I say I borrowed the money? I might have had an admirer, I might have been given it, I am quite attractive —

MRS. LINDE: You are mad —

NORA: And you're dying of curiosity, Kristine.

MRS. LINDE: Nora, my dear, have you done something foolish —

NORA: Foolish, to save your husband's life, is that foolish?

MRS. LINDE: I think it is foolish if you did something and didn't tell him about it —

NORA: No, no, you don't understand! He wasn't allowed to know how ill he was. The doctors told me. Nothing could save him, unless we travelled south. Honestly I did try and coax him at first. I tried everything. Nothing worked. Well then I thought, you have to be saved. I have to save you and I found a way out —

MRS. LINDE: You've never breathed a word since to your husband.

NORA: Oh no. When it comes to money Torvald is very strict and he absolutely loathes debt, and anyway, Torvald is a man. He has a man's pride. He would be so ashamed and humiliated if he thought he owed me anything. It would spoil our lovely marriage. It would just spoil everything.

MRS. LINDE: Will you never tell him?

NORA: I might, yes, one day. Many years from now, when I've lost my looks a little. Don't laugh. I mean the time will come when Torvald is not as in love with me as he is now, not quite so happy when I dance for him, and dress for him, and play with him. It might be useful then to have something up my sleeve — I'm talking nonsense, nonsense, that time will never come. So what do you think of my big secret? I am good for something, aren't I. But the whole affair caused me such a lot of worry. I've all these repayments and they're so hard to find. You see I couldn't really put any of the housekeeping money aside because Torvald has to live well, and I couldn't let the children go badly dressed. Whatever I got for them I had to spend it on them. Mummy's little angels.

MRS. LINDE: So the money came out of your own allowance, Nora?

NORA: Yes. When Torvald gave me money for new dresses and things, I never spent more than half. Bought the cheapest of materials. Thank goodness everything looks good on me, Torvald never even noticed. But Kristine, it was a bit hard on me. It is nice being beautifully dressed, isn't it?

MRS. LINDE: Isn't it, yes?

NORA: I found other ways of making money, as well. Last Christmas I was lucky enough to get a lot of copying to do. Can you believe that? I locked myself in my room every evening for three whole weeks, and I wrote till late at night. I was tired. So tired. I did get such a lot of pleasure from sitting and working and earning money. I felt like a man.

MRS. LINDE: How much have you paid off doing this?

NORA: I can't tell you exactly. I do know that what I've scraped together, I've paid it all. So many times I've been at my wits' end. But that's all over now. I'm free, and I can't tell you how good that feels. I can spend all my time playing with the children. I can have the house just the way Torvald likes it. Really beautiful. *(The bell is heard in the hall and Mrs. Linde gets up.)*

MRS. LINDE: Visitors. I'd better leave.

NORA: Stay, please. I'm not expecting anybody. It'll be for Torvald — *(The Maid is in the doorway to the hall.)*

MAID: Excuse me, Mrs. Helmer, a gentleman wants to go into the lawyer's office —

NORA: The bank manager's office, you mean.

MAID: Yes, the bank manager's office, but the doctor is still in there —

NORA: Ask him in. I'm sorry. *(Krogstad is in the doorway to the hall.)*

KROGSTAD: It's just me, Mrs. Helmer. *(Mrs. Linde frowns, starts, and half turns towards the window. Nora takes a step towards him, tense, and lowers her voice.)*

NORA: What do you want to talk to my husband about?

KROGSTAD: Bank business, you might say. I've got a position in the Joint Stock Bank. I now hear your husband is to be our manager.

NORA: That's right —

KROGSTAD: Yes, I merely wish to bore him with bank business. Nothing else.

NORA: Please use the study door. *(She takes her leave of him indifferently as she closes the door to the hall and goes to see to the stove.)*

MRS. LINDE: Who was that, Nora?

NORA: Mr. Krogstad. A lawyer.

MRS. LINDE: It was him then.

NORA: You know that man?

MRS. LINDE: I did — years ago. He was clerk to our local solicitor.

NORA: Yes, that's what he was.

MRS. LINDE: He's changed an awful lot.

NORA: He had a very unhappy marriage, I believe.

MRS. LINDE: Is he a widower now?

NORA: With lots of children.

MRS. LINDE: I've heard he has some dubious business interests.

NORA: Really? Well business is so boring, let's not talk about it.

(Dr. Rank enters from Helmer's study. He speaks in the doorway.)

RANK: I won't disturb you, my friend. I'll pop in and see your wife. *(He closes the door and remarks to Mrs. Linde.)* I'm so sorry, I'm disturbing you as well.

NORA: You are not. Dr. Rank, this is Mrs. Linde.

RANK: I see. I've heard that name often in this house. Didn't I pass you on the stairs coming up?

MRS. LINDE: You did. I walk slowly. Stairs tire me.

RANK: You're not feeling well?

MRS. LINDE: Tired. Just tired.

RANK: Is that all? And you come to visit in town to get back your energy?

MRS. LINDE: To get work, that's why I'm in town.

RANK: Work is now a cure for tiredness?

MRS. LINDE: One has to live, Doctor.

RANK: Yes, that's the general opinion.

NORA: Come on, Dr. Rank, you must want to live as well.

RANK: I do, indeed. I may be a miserable fellow, but I'll go on being tormented for as long as possible. All my patients feel the same way. And people who are morally sick, they do as well. Right now one of them is in there with Helmer —

MRS. LINDE: What?

NORA: What do you mean?

RANK: Krogstad. A lawyer. A man you don't know. A man rotten to the core, Madam. But he too is insisting he has to live, as if it mattered so much, his life.

NORA: What's he talking to Torvald about?

RANK: I do not know. Something to do with the Savings Bank.

NORA: Does Krog — does this lawyer, Krogstad, have anything to do with the bank?

RANK: He works there, yes, in some manner of description. You're laughing, why?

NORA: Tell me, Dr. Rank. Will everyone who works at the Savings Bank, will they all now be under Torvald?

RANK: Yes, I suppose so. Why is that so very amusing?

NORA: It gives me such pleasure to think that we — that Torvald has so much power over so many people. *(She takes a bag out of her pocket.)* A little macaroon, Dr. Rank?

RANK: What is this? Macaroons? Aren't they illegal in this house?

NORA: They are, but Kristine gave me these.

MRS. LINDE: Me — what —

NORA: Now, now don't get hysterical. You didn't know that Torvald's banned them. No. He thinks they're very bad for my teeth. Never mind — just a little one. Yes, Dr. Rank? Here you are. *(She puts a macaroon into his mouth.)* You too, Kristine. And one for me. Just a little one. Two, at most. Oh, I'm such a happy woman. There is only one thing that I want to do.

RANK: What is it?

NORA: I'd really like to say something to Torvald —

RANK: Then say it.

NORA: I daren't. It's vulgar.

MRS. LINDE: Vulgar?

RANK: Then don't. But say it to us — you can surely. What do you want to say to Helmer?

NORA: Bloody hell.

RANK: Have you gone mad?

MRS. LINDE: Nora, God help us —

RANK: Say it, he's here. *(Nora hides the bag of macaroons.)*

NORA: Quiet. *(Torvald enters from his study with his coat over his arm and his hat in his hand.)* You got rid of him, did you, Torvald dear?

HELMER: He's gone now, yes!

NORA: Introductions. This is Kristine, who's come to town.

HELMER: Kristine? Forgive me, I'm not sure —

NORA: Mrs. Linde. Mrs. Kristine Linde, darling.

HELMER: I see. You and my wife were friends as children?

MRS. LINDE: Yes, we knew each other a long time ago.

NORA: And she has travelled a long way here just to speak to you, imagine that.

HELMER: What is that supposed to mean?

MRS. LINDE: It's not exactly —

NORA: You see, Kristine's very good at office work but she really wants to work with a clever man who will teach her much more than she already knows and direct her —

HELMER: A sensible decision, Madame.

NORA: So when she heard, through a telegram, that you had become manager of the bank, she raced here as quickly as she could — please, Torvald, for my sake, could you do something for Kristine? Please, please?

HELMER: That is not impossible. I take it you are a widow?

MRS. LINDE: Yes.

HELMER: And have some experience of bookkeeping?

MRS. LINDE: A great deal, yes.

HELMER: Then it's quite likely I can offer you a position — *(Nora claps her hands.)*

NORA: I knew, I knew.

HELMER: You've arrived at the right time, Mrs. Linde —

MRS. LINDE: How can I thank you —

HELMER: No need whatsoever. *(He puts on his overcoat.)* But for now you must excuse me today —

RANK: Wait, I'll go with you. *(He fetches his fur coat from the hall and warms it by the stove.)*

NORA: Torvald my dear, don't stay out long.

HELMER: An hour. No more.

NORA: Kristine, are you leaving as well? *(Mrs. Linde puts her coat on.)*

MRS. LINDE: Yes, I now have to start searching for lodgings.

HELMER: Perhaps we can walk some of the way together. *(Nora helps her.)*

NORA: I'm so sorry that we're so cramped for space. We just could not —

MRS. LINDE: Don't even think about it. I can't thank you enough. Good-bye.

NORA: For now, good-bye. But you will come back this evening, won't you? You too, Dr. Rank. What do you say? Are you well enough? You will be, I know. Just wrap up well. *(During this conversation they enter the hall and children's voices are heard outside the door.)* Here they are, here they are. *(She runs to open the door and the Nanny, Anne-Marie, enters with the children.)* Come on, come in. *(Nora bends down and kisses the children.)* Aren't they sweet? Aren't they angels? Do you see them, Kristine? Aren't they lovely?

RANK: Stop talking in this draught.

HELMER: Come along, Mrs. Linde. Only a mother could bear to be here. *(Rank, Helmer, and Mrs. Linde go down the stairs. The Nanny enters the room with the children. Nora does so too and closes the hall door.)*

NORA: Look at those rosy red cheeks. You look so lovely I could eat you. *(The children all talk at the same time and interrupt her during the following.)* Was it great fun? Good, good. You pulled both Emmy and Bob in the sledge. Imagine that, the two of them at the same time? You're a big boy, Ivar. Anne-Marie, let me hold her a moment. My little doll, my sweet baby. *(She takes the youngest from the nanny and dances with her.)* Yes, yes, Bob, Mummy will dance with you as well. What? Snowballs, I should have seen you throw them. Anne-Marie, I'll take off their coats myself, please don't — yes, let me please. It is great fun. You look frozen to the bone. Go in there and drink some hot coffee — it's on the stove in the nursery. *(The Nanny enters the room stage L. Nora takes off the children's coats and throws them anywhere while she lets them chatter simultaneously.)* I see, a big bad dog chased you. Did it bite? No, it wouldn't. Doggies don't bite lovely baby dolls. Ivar, leave those parcels. What's in them? You would like to know. Well, it's something horrid. So, what will we play? What do you want to play? Hide and seek? Yes, hide and seek. Bob hides first. Me, will I hide first? All right, I'll hide *(There is joy as Nora and the children laugh and play. Nora finally hides under the table. The children storm in, look, cannot find her, hear her giggling, rush to the table, lift up the cloth and see her. There is huge excitement. There is a knock on the front door but no one notices. The door half-opens and Krogstad appears. He waits a little and the game continues.)*

KROGSTAD: I beg your pardon, Mrs. Helmer — *(With a stifled scream Nora starts and turns.)*

NORA: What? What do you want?

KROGSTAD: I'm sorry, the front door was open, someone must have forgotten to shut it — *(Nora gets up.)*

NORA: My husband is not at home, Mr. Krogstad.

KROGSTAD: I know.

NORA: So what do you want here then?

KROGSTAD: A word with you.

NORA: With — *(She speaks to the children who have grown quiet.)* Let's go and find Nanny shall we?

IVAR: Mummy who is that gentleman?

NORA: Just somebody who works at Daddy's new bank. *(She leads the children into the room stage L. and shuts the door. She is tense and uneasy.)* You want to talk to me?

KROGSTAD: Yes, I want to talk to you.

NORA: Why? Today isn't the first of the month —

KROGSTAD: No, it's Christmas Eve. It all depends on you whether or not you have a happy Christmas.

NORA: Today I can't possibly —

KROGSTAD: Leave that aside. I want something else. Have you a moment to spare?

NORA: Yes, I do, I believe, but —

KROGSTAD: Good. I was sitting in Olsen's cafe and saw your husband go down the street —

NORA: Yes.

KROGSTAD: With a lady.

NORA: So?

KROGSTAD: May I ask if that lady was a Mrs. Linde?

NORA: Yes.

KROGSTAD: Just come to town?

NORA: Today, yes.

KROGSTAD: Isn't she a good friend of yours?

NORA: She is yes, but why —

KROGSTAD: I thought so. All right, so I'll ask you straight out — will Mrs. Linde have a position in the Joint Stock Bank?

NORA: Mr. Krogstad, how dare you question me? You are an employee of my husband. But since you've asked, I'll answer. Yes, Mrs. Linde will have a position. And Mr. Krogstad, I spoke up for her. Now you know.

KROGSTAD: I was right then.

NORA: I do have a little bit of influence. Just because I'm a woman, it doesn't mean — that — Mr. Krogstad, you should be careful — people in a junior position should be careful not to offend people who ... who....

KROGSTAD: Who have influence —

NORA: Exactly. *(Krogstad changes his tone.)*

KROGSTAD: Mrs. Helmer, would you please be good enough to use your influence on my behalf?

NORA: What do you mean?

KROGSTAD: Would you be kind enough to make sure that I keep my junior position in the bank?

NORA: What are you talking about? Who's thinking of taking it from you?

KROGSTAD: You don't need to pretend that you don't understand.

NORA: I assure you —

KROGSTAD: While there is still time, I advise you to use your influence to stop this.

NORA: Mr. Krogstad, I have no influence —

KROGSTAD: Have no influence? I thought you said —

NORA: I didn't mean it in that way. How can you think I have influence like that over my husband?

KROGSTAD: I know your husband, we were students together. I think the bank manager is like all married men, he can be swayed.

NORA: Mr. Krogstad, if you insult my husband, I'll have to ask you to leave.

KROGSTAD: You are a brave lady.

NORA: I am not afraid of you any longer. After New Year, I will be free of the whole thing. *(Krogstad grows more controlled.)*

KROGSTAD: Mrs. Helmer, please listen to me. If push comes to shove, I will fight with my life to keep my little job at the bank.

NORA: Yes, I can see that.

KROGSTAD: It's not just for the money. That's the least important thing about it. There's another reason. I suppose you know, everyone does, that many years ago I made a bad mistake.

NORA: I've heard something like that, yes.

KROGSTAD: It never went to court, but after that it was as though all doors were closed to me. So, I took to the business that you know about. I had to live somehow, and I honestly don't think I've been as bad as many in my trade. But now I want to get out of it. My sons are growing up. I need to win back what respectability I can in the town. That position in the bank was my first step on the ladder. Now your husband is going to kick me off that ladder back into the gutter.

NORA: But honestly, Mr. Krogstad, I don't have the power to help you.

KROGSTAD: You don't have the inclination to help me, but I have the power to force you.

NORA: You wouldn't tell my husband I owe you money?

KROGSTAD: And if I did?

NORA: That would be a shameful thing to do. *(She is about to cry.)* I'm so proud of my secret. If he heard from you in such an ugly, crude way, you would put me in such an unpleasant position.

KROGSTAD: Unpleasant? Is that all? *(Nora grows angry.)*

NORA: Do it then, go on do it. See what happens then. My husband will see what a bad man you are. You certainly won't keep your job at the bank.

KROGSTAD: I've just asked you if it's only domestic unpleasantness you're worried about?

NORA: If my husband's told, he'll immediately pay what I owe you. Then we won't have anything more to do with you. *(Krogstad takes a step closer.)*

KROGSTAD: Mrs. Helmer, listen. When your husband was ill, you came to me to borrow four thousand eight hundred kroner —

NORA: I knew no one else.

KROGSTAD: I promised to get you the money.

NORA: And you did.

KROGSTAD: I promised to get you the money on certain conditions in a contract which I drew up.

NORA: You did, and I signed.

KROGSTAD: Good, but then I added another clause in which your father was to guarantee the debt. Your father was meant to sign this clause.

NORA: Meant to? He did sign.

KROGSTAD: I left the date blank. So that when your father signed the contract he could fill in the date himself. Do you remember?

NORA: I, I think so —

KROGSTAD: The amount was then paid to you.

NORA: Yes. Well, haven't I kept up the repayments?

KROGSTAD: More or less. But let's return to that date, Mrs. Helmer. Do you remember the day your father died, the day of the month, I mean?

NORA: Papa died on the twenty-ninth of September.

KROGSTAD: That's right, I checked it. *(He takes out a piece of paper.)* Which leaves us with a little problem, a problem I can't solve.

NORA: What little problem, I don't know —

KROGSTAD: The problem is Mrs. Helmer, that your father signed this contract three days after his death.

NORA: I don't understand.

KROGSTAD: Your father died on the twenty-ninth of September. But look at this. Your father has dated his signature the second of October. That is curious, isn't it? *(Nora is silent.)* Can you explain that to me? *(Nora remains silent.)* What is also remarkable is that the words "the second of October" and the year are not in your father's writing, but in writing which I seem to recognize. Nothing criminal in that. It is the signature that's important. Mrs. Helmer, that signature, is it genuine? It really was your father himself who signed his name here? *(After a brief silence Nora tosses her head and answers him defiantly.)*

NORA: No, he didn't. I signed Papa's name.

KROGSTAD: Do you realize how dangerous this admission is?

NORA: Why? You'll soon get your money.

KROGSTAD: Why didn't you send the contract to your father?

NORA: I couldn't. Papa was ill. How could I possibly tell him that my husband's life was in danger when he was so ill himself?

KROGSTAD: It would have been advisable to abandon your trip abroad.

NORA: That trip was to save my husband's life. I couldn't abandon it.

KROGSTAD: Didn't it occur to you that you were defrauding me?

NORA: I couldn't worry about that. I didn't love you.

KROGSTAD: Mrs. Helmer, I don't think you have any idea of what it is you're guilty of. But, let me tell you, my one mistake that destroyed my entire reputation was nothing more or nothing worse than what you have done.

NORA: Are you — you trying to make me believe you did something brave to save your wife's life?

KROGSTAD: The law has no interest in motives.

NORA: Then the law is very foolish.

KROGSTAD: Foolish or not, if I were to present this paper to the court, you would be judged by that law.

NORA: I don't believe that. A daughter can't protect her old, dying father? A wife can't help save her husband's life? I don't know the law very well, but I'm sure it must say somewhere that this is allowed. And if you don't know that, Mr. Krogstad, you must be a very bad lawyer.

KROGSTAD: Be that as it may, but I do know about business, and you know that. And I'll tell you one thing. You have everything to lose, your entire future, everything. If I am hurled back into the gutter a second time, I will take you with me. (*He exits through the hall. Nora, pensive for a while, tosses her head.*)

NORA: Rubbish. Trying to frighten me. I'm not that simple. (*She starts folding the children's clothes but soon stops.*) But — no, it is impossible. I did it for love. (*The children are in the doorway stage L.*)

CHILDREN: The strange man has left now, Mummy.

NORA: Yes, I know, yes. Now don't tell anyone about the strange man. Not even Daddy.

CHILDREN: No Mummy, will you play with us again?

NORA: No! No. Not now.

CHILDREN: Mummy, you promised.

NORA: Yes, but I can't now. I have so much to do. Go along, darlings, go along. (*She urges them gently out of the room and closes the door behind them. She sits down on the sofa, takes up her embroidery and sews a few stitches but soon stops.*) No. (*She throws the embroidery aside, gets up, goes to the hall door and shouts.*) Helene, could you bring in the Christmas tree, please. (*She goes to the table stage L. and opens the drawer but stops again.*) No, it is all quite impossible. (*Helene enters with the Christmas tree.*)

MAID: Where will I leave it, Madame?

NORA: The middle of the floor.

MAID: Shall I fetch anything else?

NORA: No, thank you, I have what I need. (*The Maid exits and Nora starts to decorate the tree.*) Candles, and flowers, here and here. That horrible man. Nonsense, all nonsense. Nothing is wrong. The Christmas tree will be lovely. Anything you want, Torvald, I will do. I will sing for you, dance — (*Helmer enters from the hall with a bundle of papers under his arm.*) Oh, you're back then?

HELMER: Yes. Did anyone call?

NORA: Here? No.

HELMER: Strange. I saw Krogstad coming out the front door downstairs.

NORA: Oh? Yes, that's true, Krogstad was here for a moment.

HELMER: Nora, I can read you like a book, he was here asking you to put in a good word for him.

NORA: Yes.

HELMER: And you were told not to tell me he'd been. That's what he's asked you to do, yes?

NORA: Yes, Torvald, but —

HELMER: Nora, how could you agree to that? How, Nora? You talk to a man like that, and make him promises. Then, to top it all, you tell me a lie.

NORA: Lie?

HELMER: Didn't you say no one had been here? *(He wags his finger.)* My singing bird must never again do that. This little bird must keep its voice pure. No false notes. *(He puts his hands around her waist.)* That's so, yes? Yes, I thought so. *(He lets her go.)* So, no more about it. *(He sits down in front of the stove.)* It's so warm and cozy in here. *(He leafs through the papers. Nora busies herself with the tree. There is a short pause.)*

NORA: What are those papers?

HELMER: Bank business.

NORA: Already?

HELMER: I've persuaded the retiring manager to give me authority to change staff and policy. By New Year I want everything in order.

NORA: So that's why this poor Krogstad —

HELMER: Hmm. *(Nora is still over the back of the chair, slowly messing up his hair.)*

NORA: Well, if you hadn't been terribly busy, I would have asked you a really, really big favor, Torvald?

HELMER: Spell it out, what is it?

NORA: No one has better taste than you. I so want to look good at the fancy dress party at the Sternborgs tomorrow night. Torvald, would you tell me what my costume should be?

HELMER: Little Miss Stubbornshoes needs to be helped?

NORA: I do, Torvald, I can't get anywhere without your help.

HELMER: All right, I'll think about it. We'll come up with something.

NORA: You are kind. *(She goes back to the Christmas tree. There is a pause.)* Tell me, this Krogstad, was what he did so terribly bad?

HELMER: He forged a signature. Have you any idea what that means?

NORA: Perhaps he did it because he desperately needed to?

HELMER: He could have, or because he was reckless, like so many others. That's not the point, Nora. I'm not heartless, I condemn no man outright for one mistake.

NORA: No, you wouldn't, Torvald.

HELMER: Anyone can save himself if he admits his guilt and takes the punishment.

NORA: What punishment?

HELMER: Forgery is punishable by imprisonment. But Krogstad tricked his way out of it with lies and deceit. A guilty man has to lie to everyone. Absolutely everyone, his nearest and his dearest, his wife and his children. Nora, they have never seen the real man, behind that mask. And the children, Nora, that's what makes it so terrible.

NORA: Why?

HELMER: Every breath those children take must be filled with the germs of something evil because an atmosphere of lies infects and poisons an entire house.

NORA: Are you sure?

HELMER: I know it. I know it as a lawyer. Nearly all the young criminals I've dealt with have mothers that lied.

NORA: Just the mothers?

HELMER: No, of course not, but the mothers spend far more time with the children. Fathers can have the same effect. Krogstad has gone home for years and poisoned his children with lies and deceit, and that's why I call him an immoral man. That's why my lovely Nora must promise me now, not to plead his case any more. Give me your hand on this. What is this, Nora? Give me your hand. There, it's settled. I assure you, it would have been impossible to work with him. I honestly feel sick, sick to my stomach, in the presence of such people. *(Nora withdraws her hand and goes to the other side of the Christmas tree.)*

NORA: So hot in here — so much to do, I have — *(Helmer gets up and gathers his papers together.)*

HELMER: Yes, I'm thinking of reading some of this before dinner. I'll have to give your costume a bit of thought. And I might have to wrap something in gold paper on the Christmas tree. *(He puts his hand on her head.)* It's going to be a beautiful Christmas with the children. *(He enters the study, closing the door behind him. Nora speaks quietly after a pause.)*

NORA: No, it's not possible. It isn't. *(The Nanny appears in the doorway stage L.)*

NANNY: Your little ones ask very sweetly if they can come to Mummy.

NORA: No, absolutely no, don't let them near me. Keep them away from me.

NANNY: Very well, Mrs. Helmer. *(She closes the door. Nora pales from fear.)*

NORA: Poison my children — poison my home — poison them — *(There is a brief pause. She raises her head.)* It is not true. Never, never, never ever could it be true.

ACT TWO

The same living room. In the corner by the piano the Christmas tree stands, stripped of presents, dishevelled, and with the remains of burned down candles. Nora's coat lies on the sofa.

Nora is alone, pacing the living room floor uneasily, until she finally stops by the sofa and picks up her coat. She lets go of her coat.

NORA: Somebody's coming. *(She turns towards the door and listens.)* Nobody — nobody. Christmas Day, no one will come today. Nor tomorrow either. But maybe — *(She opens the door and looks out.)* Nothing in the post box. Nothing. Empty. *(She walks the floor.)* You're being ridiculous. He won't do it of course. Something like this, it can't happen. It's impossible. I have little children. *(Nanny enters from the room stage L. with a big cardboard box.)*

NANNY: Well I've come across the box with the costumes at last.

NORA: Thank you. Put it down there. *(She does so.)* I'll go out and get Mrs. Linde to give me a hand.

NANNY: Go out again, you? In this bad weather? You'll get a cold, you'll end up in bed, Mrs. Helmer.

NORA: Worse could happen. How are the children?

NANNY: The poor darlings are playing with their Christmas presents, but —

NORA: Are they still asking for me?

NANNY: They're so used to having their Mummy with them.

NORA: Yes, but Anne-Marie, from now on I can't be with them as much as I have been.

NANNY: Little children, they get used to nearly everything.

NORA: Do you think so? Do you think they would forget their mother if she went away forever?

NANNY: Dear me, forever?

NORA: Dear Anne-Marie, you were such a good nanny to me when I was a child.

NANNY: Poor child, little Nora had no other mother but me.

NORA: And if the children had no one else, I know that you — you — this is not making sense, I'm talking nonsense, nonsense. *(She opens the box.)* Go to them. Now I have to — Tomorrow, you'll see how beautiful I'll look.

NANNY: Yes. Mrs. Nora will be the loveliest lady at the party. *(She exits to the room stage L. Nora starts to unpack the box but soon throws everything down.)*

NORA: Maybe if I dared go out. I'll brush this muff. Gorgeous, gorgeous. Don't think about it, forget — one, two, three, four, five, six — *(She screams.)* They're coming — *(She wants to move towards the door but stands indecisively. Mrs. Linde enters from the hall where she's left her outdoor clothes.)* Kristine, is that you? Is there anyone else out there? I'm glad that it's you who came.

MRS. LINDE: I heard you'd come by asking for me.

NORA: Yes, I was just passing. You must help me with something. Sit down on the sofa. Look. There is a fancy dress party at the Sternborgs tomorrow evening. Torvald wants me to go as a fisher girl from Naples and dance the tarantella. I learnt it in Capri.

MRS. LINDE: I see. You're going to give a real performance?

NORA: Torvald wants me to. Here's the costume, look — it's falling to pieces and I just don't know —

MRS. LINDE: We'll soon mend it. The trimming is hanging down in a few places. Needle and thread? Right, we have what we need.

NORA: This is kind of you. *(Mrs. Linde sews.)*

MRS. LINDE: But I'm forgetting to say thank you for the lovely evening last night. *(Nora gets up and walks across the floor.)*

NORA: It wasn't quite as lovely here last night as it usually is.

MRS. LINDE: Tell me, is Dr. Rank normally as miserable as he was last night?

NORA: No. Yesterday, it was very noticeable. You see, he suffers from a very serious illness. Poor man, his spine is wasting away:

his father was a brute of a man. He had mistresses — things of that nature. So the son was infected from boyhood, inherited — if you follow me. *(Mrs. Linde lets the sewing drop.)*

MRS. LINDE: My darling Nora, how did you come to know such things? *(Nora strolls.)*

NORA: When you have given birth to three children, you get visits from — from ladies who possess some medical knowledge. They can tell you a thing or two, I can tell you.

MRS. LINDE: Nora, listen, you're still a child in many ways. I'm a bit older than you and have a bit more experience. I want to tell you something. You must stop all this business with Dr. Rank.

NORA: Stop what business?

MRS. LINDE: Nora, stop pretending. Don't you realize I've guessed who loaned you the money?

NORA: Have you gone mad? How could you think of such a thing? He is a friend, who comes here every single day. That would be terribly embarrassing. Mind you I'm certain if I were to ask —

MRS. LINDE: You won't though, naturally.

NORA: No, naturally. I don't think it would be necessary. But I'm sure if I told Dr. Rank —

MRS. LINDE: Behind your husband's back?

NORA: This other thing was behind his back too, and I have to get out of it. I have to get out of it!

MRS. LINDE: That's what I said to you yesterday, but — *(She stops.)*

NORA: When you pay up what you owe, you get your contract back, don't you?

MRS. LINDE: That's correct, yes.

NORA: Then you can tear it up into a hundred thousand pieces and burn it — that nasty, disgusting piece of paper. *(Mrs. Linde puts down the sewing, gets up slowly, and looks at Nora sternly.)*

MRS. LINDE: What is it, Nora? Something's happened to you since yesterday morning. *(Nora goes towards her.)*

NORA: Kristine. *(She listens.)* Ssh. Torvald's come home. Kristine, would you mind taking the sewing in there? Torvald hates the sight of sewing. Let Anne-Marie help you. *(Mrs. Linde gathers up some items.)*

MRS. LINDE: All right, but I'm not leaving until we've spoken honestly. *(Mrs. Linde exits stage L. at the same time as Helmer enters from the hall. Nora goes to meet him.)*

NORA: Torvald, I've missed you so much.

HELMER: Was that the dressmaker?

NORA: No. Kristine, she's helping me mend my costume. Don't worry, I'll look beautiful for you.

HELMER: Yes, that was a rather clever idea of mine.

NORA: Wonderful. But aren't I good to give in to you? *(Helmer lifts her chin.)*

HELMER: Good — because you give in to your husband? You funny little thing. I know you didn't mean it like that. Go on, I won't trouble you. I imagine you want to try it on.

NORA: And I imagine you need to work?

HELMER: Yes. *(He shows her a bundle of papers.)* Look, I've been to the bank — *(He is about to enter his study.)*

NORA: Torvald. *(He stops.)*

HELMER: Yes.

NORA: Say your little bird were to ask you for something very prettily —

HELMER: What?

NORA: Would you do it?

HELMER: I would have to know what it is first.

NORA: Your skylark would sing in all the rooms —

HELMER: So? My skylark does that anyway.

NORA: I'd work magic in the moonlight and dance for you, Torvald.

HELMER: Nora, surely this hasn't anything to do with what you mentioned this morning? *(Nora moves closer.)*

NORA: Yes. I beg you with all my heart, Torvald.

HELMER: You really have the nerve to bring this up again?

NORA: Yes, you must do as I ask, please, you must let Krogstad keep his job at the bank.

HELMER: I've decided to give his job to Mrs. Linde, dear Nora.

NORA: That is very, very kind of you. But couldn't you get rid of another clerk instead of Krogstad?

HELMER: I do not believe how stubborn you are. Just because you've made him a foolish promise, you are making me —

NORA: That's not the reason, Torvald.

HELMER: What is it then?

NORA: I'm only thinking about you. The man writes in the most dreadful newspapers. You've said that yourself. He can do you untold harm. I'm frightened to death of him.

HELMER: You're frightened by old memories. Your father — that's who you're thinking about.

NORA: I am, yes. I am. People wrote such wicked things about Papa in the papers. Remember that. They slandered him so viciously. I'm sure he would have been dismissed if they hadn't sent you to look into it. You were so kind, you helped him so much.

HELMER: My little Nora, there is a very big difference between your father and myself. As a civil servant your father's reputation was not beyond reproach. Mine is. And I hope it will remain so, for as long as I hold my position.

NORA: But you never know what harm people can do. We could be so comfortable now, so content, so happy in our peaceful home — you and me and the children, Torvald. That is why I really do beg you —

HELMER: The more you plead for this man, the more impossible it is for me to keep him. Everyone in the bank knows I'm going to get rid of Krogstad. If word got about that the new bank manager let his wife change his mind —

NORA: So, what then, yes?

HELMER: I'll tell you what then. If little Miss Stubbornshoes gets her way, I'd be made a laughing stock before the entire staff. People would start to think I didn't have a mind of my own. Believe you me, I'd soon have to face the consequences. Anyway, there is another reason why it is quite impossible for Krogstad to stay in the bank while I am manager.

NORA: What?

HELMER: If I were pushed to it, I could overlook his moral failings —

NORA: Yes, you could, Torvald.

HELMER: I'm told he could be quite useful. But we've known each other from being students together. It's one of those ill-judged friendships that so often come back to haunt you. I'm telling you the truth now. We call each other by our christian

35

names. But this man has no tact, he continues to do so even when other people are present. In fact, he thinks he has a right, to be very familiar with me. He keeps interrupting all the time with "Torvald this," "Torvald that." It's so embarrassing. He would make my position at the bank absolutely impossible.

NORA: You can't mean this, Torvald.

HELMER: Why can't I?

NORA: Because it's such a petty reason.

HELMER: Petty? What are you saying? You think I'm petty?

NORA: I don't, Torvald. Darling, this is precisely why —

HELMER: Never mind that. You just said my reason is petty, that means I am petty too. Petty. Never — I — I can put an end to all of this. *(He goes to the hall door and shouts.)* Helene.

NORA: What are you going to do? *(Helmer looks through his papers.)*

HELMER: To settle this once and for all. *(The Maid enters.)* This letter, take it. Go downstairs, find a messenger, and tell him to deliver it. Do it quickly. The address is on the envelope. Here's some money.

MAID: Yes, sir. *(The Maid leaves with the letter. He tidies up his papers.)*

HELMER: There you have it, little Miss Stubbornshoes. *(Nora speaks breathlessly.)*

NORA: Torvald — what was that letter?

HELMER: Krogstad's dismissal.

NORA: Torvald, get it back. There's still time. You don't know what this could do to our family.

HELMER: It's too late.

NORA: Too late, yes.

HELMER: Dear Nora, I can forgive you because you are frightened, though actually it's an insult to think I would be frightened because some failed, depraved hack wants revenge against me. But I forgive you, anyway, because this shows me, how beautifully, and how bravely you love me. *(He takes her in his arms.)* Whatever happens, when a real crisis comes, you'll see, I have strength and courage for both of us. You'll see that I'm man enough to deal with everything myself. *(Nora is terrified.)*

NORA: What do you mean by that?

HELMER: Everything I say. *(Nora grows composed.)*

NORA: You will never, ever have to do that.

HELMER: Good. Then we'll share everything, Nora — as man and wife. As it should be. *(He caresses her.)* Happy now? There, there, there, don't show me those frightened eyes, my dove. It's all in your imagination. Now you ought to practice the tarantella, with the tambourine. I'll go to the study and close the door, so I won't hear anything. You can make as much noise as you like. *(He turns around in the doorway.)* When Rank comes, tell him where I am. *(He nods to her, goes with his papers to his study and closes the door. Nora stands rooted to the floor, despairing with anxiety, and whispers.)*

NORA: He is capable of doing it. He will do it. He will do it, no matter what. No, never, never ever. Never, never. Save me — a way out — *(The bell rings in the hall.)* Dr. Rank! Anything rather than that — I won't let you take the blame for me. *(She wipes her face, pulls herself together and goes to open the door to the hall. Dr. Rank stands outside and is hanging up his fur coat. During their conversation it begins to grow dark.)* Dr. Rank, it's you. Don't go into Torvald yet, I believe he's busy.

RANK: And you? *(He enters the room and she closes the door behind him.)*

NORA: Me? You know I always have time to spare for Dr. Rank.

RANK: Thank you. I'll enjoy that for as long as I can.

NORA: As long as you can? What do you mean?

RANK: Does that frighten you?

NORA: It's a curious expression. What could happen?

RANK: I've long been prepared for what could happen. I simply didn't think it would happen so soon. *(Nora clasps his arms.)*

NORA: What have you been told? Tell me, Dr. Rank. *(Rank sits down by the stove.)*

RANK: I'm going downhill, and nothing's to be done. *(Nora breathes a sigh of relief.)*

NORA: So it's you —

RANK: It's pointless lying to myself. Within a month I may be rotting in the churchyard. I've a few more tests to do. When I've done that, I should know when the disintegration begins.

NORA: That's a hideous thing to say.

RANK: There is something I want to tell you. Helmer cannot face up to anything ugly. I don't want him in my sick room —

NORA: Dr. Rank, please —

RANK: I don't want him there. Absolutely not. I'll lock my door to him, as soon as I know the very worst. When I send my visiting card to you, with a black cross on it, you'll know then that my terrible death has come calling. You'll soon get over the loss. Those out of sight are soon out of mind.

NORA: Good heavens, you are being unreasonable. *(Nora sits down on the sofa.)* Dr. Rank, please be nice. You'll see, tomorrow how beautifully I can dance. You must imagine I dance only for you — and for Torvald as well — that goes without saying. *(She takes various items from the box.)* Dr. Rank, sit down. I've something to show you. *(She sits down.)*

RANK: What is it? Silk stockings.

NORA: Lovely, aren't they? The color of flesh. No, no, no. Only the foot. Well, I'll allow you to look a little higher.

RANK: Well.

NORA: You look so disapproving — why? Do you think they may not fit?

RANK: I do not know, I don't possess that information. *(She looks at him for a moment.)*

NORA: Shame, shame. *(She hits him lightly on the ear with the stockings.)* That will teach you. *(She packs them away again.)*

RANK: What other beauties shall I get to see?

NORA: You won't get to see anything more, because you are a bold boy. *(She hums a little and searches among the items. There is a short pause.)*

RANK: When we sit like this, like intimates, I cannot understand — cannot comprehend what would have become of me if I had never entered this house. *(Nora smiles.)*

NORA: Yes, you like being with us, don't you? *(Rank looks away and speaks more quietly.)*

RANK: And to leave it all, to have to leave —

NORA: Nonsense, you won't leave. *(Rank continues in the same tone.)*

RANK: To leave no token of thanks behind. To be barely missed.

NORA: If I were to ask you — nothing.

RANK: What?

NORA: For a great proof of your friendship —

RANK: Would you really make me so happy?

NORA: You don't even know what it is.

RANK: Then ask it.

NORA: I can't. It's too much — far too much. I need advice and help, I need a favor —

RANK: All you ask for. Don't you trust me?

NORA: Of course I do. Dr. Rank, this is something you must help me stop happening. You know how much Torvald loves me — how unbelievably much he loves me. There isn't a moment when he wouldn't give his life for me. *(Rank leans towards her.)*

RANK: Nora, do you think he is the only one — *(Nora jolts lightly.)*

NORA: What?

RANK: Who would gladly give his life for you? I swore to myself that you would know this before I'd go away. I will never find a better opportunity. Yes, now you know, Nora. And now you always know that you can trust me as you can trust no one else. *(Nora rises. Rank remains seated but makes room for her.)* Nora — *(Nora stands in the door to the hall.)*

NORA: Helene, are you back?

HELENE: *(Off.)* Yes, Mrs. Helmer. *(Nora goes to the stove.)*

NORA: Can you bring in the lamp? That was extremely wicked of you, Dr. Rank. *(He gets up.)*

RANK: Wicked? To have loved you as deeply as any other —

NORA: Wicked to have gone and told me. It was not necessary —

RANK: What do you mean? Did you know — *(The Maid enters with the lamp, puts it on the table and exits.)* I'm asking you, Nora, Mrs. Helmer, did you know something?

NORA: Did I know, did I not know — what of it?

RANK: At least you know now for sure that I'm absolutely yours, body and soul. And will you now ask? *(Nora looks at him.)*

NORA: After this?

RANK: Don't punish me like this. I'll do what is humanly possible, if you'll let me.

NORA: What can you do for me now? Nothing. Anyway, it's all in my imagination. All in my imagination. Naturally. *(She sits in the rocking chair, looks at him and smiles.)* Well, Dr. Rank, aren't you just a little bit ashamed, now the lamp has come in?

RANK: I'm not, no. Should I leave — for good?

NORA: You mustn't do that, no. You must come here every day

just as you always do. You know very well that Torvald can't do without you.

RANK: Can you?

NORA: I do think it is great fun when you're here.

RANK: That's exactly what I misinterpreted. You're a mystery to me. Often it seems to me you prefer my company almost as much as Helmer's.

NORA: You see, there are people who one loves and then there are others whose company one almost prefers.

RANK: There is something in that.

NORA: When I lived at home, I loved Papa more than anyone else in the world, but I always thought it great fun to hide downstairs with the maids. They didn't tell me what to do all the time, and they had such a good time together.

RANK: And I have now taken the place of the maids. *(Nora jumps up and goes to him.)*

NORA: Dear kind Dr. Rank, that was not what I meant at all. But you can imagine being with Torvald is a little bit like being with Papa. *(The Maid enters from the hall.)*

MAID: Mrs. Helmer. *(She whispers and hands her a visiting card. Nora glances at the card.)*

NORA: Oh! *(She puts it in her pocket.)*

RANK: Is something wrong?

NORA: Nothing whatsoever. Something — something about my new costume —

RANK: Your costume's over there.

NORA: It is, yes. This is another I've ordered. Torvald mustn't know —

RANK: The great secret is revealed.

NORA: Yes. Would you do me a favor? He's in the study. Keep him busy for a while —

RANK: Worry not. He won't escape from me. *(He enters Helmer's study. Nora addresses the Maid.)*

NORA: Is he waiting in the kitchen?

MAID: And he won't leave until he's spoken to you, Mrs. Helmer.

NORA: Then show him in. Do it quietly. Helene, don't breathe a word of this. He's bringing a surprise for my husband.

MAID: I understand, yes. *(She exits.)*

40

NORA: It's going to happen. No, it can't happen. It shall not happen. *(She goes and locks the door to Helmer's study. The Maid opens the door to Krogstad and closes it after him. He is, dressed in a fur coat for travelling, a fur hat, and galoshes. Nora turns towards him.)* Thank you Helene. Keep your voice down. My husband's at home.

KROGSTAD: I presume you know I've been dismissed.

NORA: Mr. Krogstad, you must believe me, you really must. I fought for you as well as I could.

KROGSTAD: Your husband can't love you very much, can he? He knows I can expose you to the world and yet he dares to dismiss me.

NORA: How can you imagine he knows anything —

KROGSTAD: Ah, I didn't think so. But since you seem so anxious to keep this matter to yourself, I presume you know a little more than yesterday what precisely you have done?

NORA: More than you could ever teach me.

KROGSTAD: Yes, a bad lawyer like me —

NORA: What is it you want from me?

KROGSTAD: Just to see how you were, Mrs. Helmer. Even money-lenders can have a little of what you call feeling, you know.

NORA: Show it then. My little children, think of them.

KROGSTAD: Have you thought of mine? Has your husband? Still, let that pass. I just want to tell you not to take this business too seriously. I am not going to make any accusation for the time being.

NORA: Oh, thank you. I know you wouldn't do anything really.

KROGSTAD: This can all be dealt with quite amicably. There's no reason why anyone else should know anything about it. It will be just between ourselves, the three of us.

NORA: No, my husband must never know anything about this.

KROGSTAD: Mrs. Helmer, you are not going to get your contract back.

NORA: What are you going to do with it?

KROGSTAD: No one else will know anything about it. I just want to keep it. So if all this has made you think of doing something desperate —

NORA: It has.

KROGSTAD: If you were thinking of running away —

41

NORA: Yes.

KROGSTAD: Or something worse —

NORA: How do you know?

KROGSTAD: Put that thought out of your mind.

NORA: How do you know I was thinking about that?

KROGSTAD: Most of us think of that first. I thought of it too. But I didn't have the courage —

NORA: Neither do I. *(Krogstad is relieved.)*

KROGSTAD: That's it, isn't it. You haven't the courage either, do you?

NORA: No, I don't. I don't.

KROGSTAD: Besides, it would be very foolish. Once the first domestic storm is over — I have a letter here in my pocket for your husband —

NORA: Telling him everything?

KROGSTAD: As delicately as possible. *(Nora speaks quickly.)*

NORA: He mustn't get that letter. Just tell me how much you want from my husband and I'll get it.

KROGSTAD: I don't want money from your husband.

NORA: What do you want?

KROGSTAD: I want to get back on my feet, Mrs. Helmer, and that's where your husband is going to help me. For the past eighteen months I've not been involved in anything untoward. All that time I've lived in extreme hardship. I want to get back into that bank again in a higher grade. Your husband will make a place for me. I'll be the bank manager's right-hand man, and within a year Nils Krogstad will run the Joint Stock Bank, *not* Torvald Helmer.

NORA: Not in your lifetime, or mine.

KROGSTAD: So you may do something —

NORA: I have the courage now.

KROGSTAD: You can't frighten me. A fine, spoilt lady —

NORA: You'll just have to wait and see.

KROGSTAD: Under the ice? Perhaps? Sinking into the black, cold water? And then in the spring floating to the surface, ugly, unrecognizable, with your hair fallen out.

NORA: You can't frighten me. *(Nora stands and looks at him, speechless.)*

KROGSTAD: I've prepared you now. I shall expect to hear from Helmer as soon as he gets my letter. And remember, it's him, your husband, who's forced me to do this kind of thing again. I will never forgive him for that. Good-bye, Mrs. Helmer. *(He exits through the hall. Nora goes towards the hall door, opens it a little and listens.)*

NORA: He's not going to give him the letter. No, he's not. Not possible. *(A letter falls into the post box. We hear Krogstad's footsteps which gradually diminish as he goes down the stairs. Nora gives a stifled cry, runs across the floor to the sofa table. There is a short pause.)* The post box. The letter's there. Torvald, Torvald — we are lost. *(Mrs. Linde enters with the costume.)*

MRS. LINDE: Nora, Nora, I've mended everything. Do you want to try it on — *(Nora speaks hoarsely, in a stifled way.)*

NORA: Kristine, come here. *(Mrs. Linde throws the clothes on the sofa.)*

MRS. LINDE: What's wrong? Why are you so upset.

NORA: Come here. Do you see that letter? Look — through the glass — in the post box.

MRS. LINDE: Yes, I can see it. Why?

NORA: A letter from Krogstad —

MRS. LINDE: Nora — it was Krogstad who lent you the money.

NORA: Yes. Now Torvald will know everything.

MRS. LINDE: Nora, believe me, this will be the best thing for you, both of you.

NORA: You don't understand. I forged a signature —

MRS. LINDE: Oh my God —

NORA: I want to tell you, Kristine, so you will be my witness.

MRS. LINDE: Witness to what?

NORA: If I go out of my mind — which may happen —

MRS. LINDE: No, Nora.

NORA: Or if anything were to happen to me — if I could not stay here any longer —

MRS. LINDE: Nora, Nora, you are not going to go out of your mind —

NORA: If someone were to take it all on himself, all the blame —

MRS. LINDE: Yes, but how can you think —

NORA: You will be my witness that it's not true, Kristine. I am not mad, I am not. I know exactly what I'm saying. And I tell you, no one else knew about it, I did it all by myself. Remember that. Promise me that.

MRS. LINDE: I will. But I don't understand this.

NORA: How could you understand? Something glorious is going to happen.

MRS. LINDE: Glorious?

NORA: A miracle, yes. But it's frightening, Kristine. It can't happen, not for anything in the world.

MRS. LINDE: Hush, hush, it's all right. You must stop crying, and listen to me. I'm going to talk to Krogstad.

NORA: Don't. He'll harm you.

MRS. LINDE: When I knew him before, he would have done anything for me.

NORA: Him?

MRS. LINDE: Yes, him. Where does he live?

NORA: How would I — yes. *(She reaches in her pocket.)* His card. But the letter, the letter — *(In his study, Helmer knocks on the door.)*

HELMER: Nora. *(Nora screams with fear.)*

NORA: What? What do you want?

HELMER: It's all right. Don't be so frightened. We won't barge in. You've locked the door. Are you trying on your costume?

NORA: Yes, that's right, my costume I'm trying it on. I'll look so beautiful, Torvald. *(Mrs. Linde has read the card.)*

MRS. LINDE: He lives just around the corner.

NORA: There's no point. We're lost. The letter is in the box.

MRS. LINDE: Does your husband have the key?

NORA: Yes, always.

MRS. LINDE: Krogstad must ask for his letter back, he must think of an excuse —

NORA: But now is just the time when Torvald —

MRS. LINDE: Delay him. Do something. Go into him. I'll be back as soon as I can. *(She exits through the hall door. Nora goes to Helmer's room, opens it and looks inside.)*

NORA: Torvald? *(He speaks from the study.)*

HELMER: So, I'm allowed back into my own drawing room, am I? Come on, Rank, let's take a look — *(He is in the doorway.)* What's this?

NORA: What, my darling?

HELMER: Rank had me all prepared for a great costume change. *(Rank is in the doorway.)*

RANK: That's what I understood. But it seems I was wrong.

NORA: Until tomorrow no one will see me in my finery.

HELMER: Nora dear, you look worn out. Have you been practicing too much?

NORA: No, I've not practiced at all.

HELMER: You will have to —

NORA: I most definitely will have to, yes, Torvald. But I'm useless without your help.

HELMER: We'll soon polish it up again.

NORA: Yes, look after me, Torvald, please. Promise me that, please? I'm so nervous. It's such a big party. You must give up your whole evening to me. Not a word about business. No pen in your hand. You will, won't you, Torvald? Promise me, promise.

HELMER: Promise. Tonight I will be wholly at your service. You helpless little thing. But first I must — *(He goes towards the hall door.)*

NORA: No, what do you want out there?

HELMER: To see if any letters have been delivered.

NORA: No, don't Torvald. No.

HELMER: What is it now?

NORA: I beg you, Torvald. There's nothing there.

HELMER: Let me see anyway. *(He makes to go. Nora, by the piano, dances the first bars of the tarantella. By the door, Helmer stops.)* Aha.

NORA: I can't dance tomorrow if I don't practice the steps for you. *(He goes to her.)*

HELMER: Are you really so nervous, darling?

NORA: I am. I am so terribly nervous. Let me rehearse now. There's still time before dinner. Torvald, please sit down and play for me. Teach me, correct me the way you usually do.

HELMER: With pleasure, if you want that, with great pleasure. We need music. *(He arranges himself at the piano. Nora takes the tambourine from the box and a long, multi-coloured shawl. She quickly throws it about herself and she springs onto the floor and shouts.)*

NORA: Dr. Rank, help me.

HELMER: A little treat for Dr. Rank. Ready?

NORA: Yes.

HELMER: And.... *(He plays and she dances. Rank stands behind Helmer at the piano and watches. Helmer continues playing.)* Good. Slow down — slow down.

NORA: I can't dance any other way.

HELMER: Nora, it's too violent.

NORA: It has to be just like this. *(Helmer stops playing.)*

HELMER: No, no, this is no good at all. *(Nora laughs and swings the tambourine.)*

NORA: What did I tell you?

RANK: Let me play for her. *(Helmer gets up.)*

HELMER: Do, please. Then I can teach her better. *(Rank sits down at the piano and plays. Nora dances more and more wildly. Helmer positions himself by the stove. During the dance Helmer keeps addressing corrective comments to Nora. She does not appear to hear them. She does not notice her hair come loose and fall over her shoulders. She keeps dancing. Mrs. Linde enters and stands as if glued to the floor. Nora calls out, still dancing.)*

NORA: Kristine, look — such fun.

HELMER: Nora, my love, you're dancing as if your life depends on it.

NORA: It does.

HELMER: Rank, stop it — this is utter insanity. I'm telling you — stop. *(Rank stops playing and Nora stops suddenly. Helmer goes to her.)* I cannot believe this — I really cannot. You've forgotten everything I taught you. What's the matter with you? *(Nora throws down the tambourine.)*

NORA: See — see.

HELMER: I see you certainly need instruction.

NORA: You must think of no one but me, not today, not tomorrow. No letters — don't even open the post box —

HELMER: Nora, a letter's already come from Krogstad, I can tell.

NORA: There may be. But don't read anything now. Nothing ugly should come between us until all this is finished. *(Rank speaks quietly to Helmer.)*

RANK: It might be wise not to cross her. *(Helmer embraces her.)*

HELMER: The child commands and I'll obey. But tomorrow evening, when you've danced —

NORA: You're free then. *(The Maid is in the door, stage R.)*

MAID: Dinner is served, Mrs. Helmer.

NORA: Champagne, we'll drink champagne.

MAID: Very well, Madam. *(She exits.)*

HELMER: I see, I see — a big party now?

NORA: Let's drink champagne till dawn. *(She shouts.)* And macaroons, Helene, a few — lots — just this once. *(Helmer takes her hands.)*

HELMER: Come on now, this excitement has upset you. Please, be my skylark again, please.

NORA: I will be. But just for now, go in there. You too, Dr. Rank. Kristine, you must help me tidy up my hair. *(Rank is subdued as they leave.)*

RANK: What is this — I mean, she's not expecting, is she?

HELMER: I don't know. *(They exit stage R.)*

NORA: Well?

MRS. LINDE: Gone to the country.

NORA: Your face said it all.

MRS. LINDE: He'll be back tomorrow night. I left him a note.

NORA: You shouldn't have. Let it all happen. It's thrilling, isn't it, waiting for something glorious to happen.

MRS. LINDE: What are you waiting for?

NORA: You wouldn't understand. Go in and join them. I'll be in in a minute. *(Mrs. Linde goes into the dining room. Nora stands awhile, collects herself, then looks at her watch.)* Five o'clock. Midnight is seven hours away. Twenty-four hours until the next midnight. The tarantella will have passed. Twenty-four and seven. Thirty-one hours to live. *(Helmer is in the door stage R.)*

HELMER: What's keeping my little skylark? *(Nora goes towards him with outstretched arms.)*

NORA: Your skylark is flying to you.

ACT THREE

The same room. The sofa table has been moved to the middle of the floor, with chairs around it. A lamp burns on the table. The door to the hall is open. Dance music can be heard from the floor above.

Mrs. Linde sits by the table and tries to read, leafing through a book, unable to concentrate. A few times she listens intently towards the hall door. She looks at her watch. She listens again. She goes to the hall and opens the door cautiously. Quiet steps can be heard on the stairs and she whispers.

MRS. LINDE: Come in, no one's here. *(Krogstad is in the doorway.)*

KROGSTAD: I found a note from you at home. What is this about?

MRS. LINDE: I have to speak to you.

KROGSTAD: Oh, have you? Does it have to be in this house?

MRS. LINDE: It is not possible at my lodgings. There's no privacy there. We're on our own. Come in. The maid's asleep and the Helmers are upstairs at a dance. *(He enters the room.)*

KROGSTAD: I see. So, the Helmers dance tonight? They're dancing?

MRS. LINDE: Why shouldn't they dance?

KROGSTAD: Absolutely. Why shouldn't they dance?

MRS. LINDE: It's time for us to talk.

KROGSTAD: Do we have anything more to talk about?

MRS. LINDE: We have a great deal to talk about.

KROGSTAD: I shouldn't have thought so.

MRS. LINDE: You wouldn't, because you have never really understood.

KROGSTAD: Was there anything to understand, except what

48

was clear to everybody? A heartless woman dumps a man when she's offered a better deal.

MRS. LINDE: Do you think I have no heart? Do you think I left you with an easy heart?

KROGSTAD: Didn't you?

MRS. LINDE: Did you really think that?

KROGSTAD: Then why did you write to me the way you did?

MRS. LINDE: What else could I do? I had to leave you, and so I had to destroy everything you felt for me. *(Krogstad clenches his fist.)*

KROGSTAD: My God, — and you did this for money.

MRS. LINDE: You mustn't forget I had a helpless mother and two younger brothers. We couldn't wait for you, Nils. Your prospects were so remote then.

KROGSTAD: Even so. But you did not have the right to throw me aside like that for someone else.

MRS. LINDE: I really don't know. I've asked myself many times if I had that right. *(Krogstad speaks more quietly.)*

KROGSTAD: When I lost you, I lost my bearings — it was as if the solid ground had given way under my feet. Look at me. Now, I'm wrecked, the ship's gone, and I'm a man clinging to wreckage.

MRS. LINDE: Help might be looking you in the face.

KROGSTAD: It was looking me in the face, but you've come and got in the way.

MRS. LINDE: I didn't know until today that I was to replace you at the bank.

KROGSTAD: But now you do know it, are you going to resign?

MRS. LINDE: No. Because it would not help you in the slightest if I did.

KROGSTAD: Well, I would have done it.

MRS. LINDE: I've learned to be practical. Life and hard bitter necessity have taught me that.

KROGSTAD: And life has taught me not to believe in fine words.

MRS. LINDE: Then life has taught you something useful. But do you believe in doing something?

KROGSTAD: What do you mean by that?

MRS. LINDE: You said you were like a shipwrecked man clinging to wreckage.

KROGSTAD: I had good reason to say that.

MRS. LINDE: Well I'm like a shipwrecked woman, clinging to the wreckage as well. I've no one to care about, no one to care for.

KROGSTAD: You made that choice yourself.

MRS. LINDE: There was no other choice then.

KROGSTAD: So, what about it?

MRS. LINDE: Nils, suppose these two shipwrecked people could reach each other?

KROGSTAD: What are you saying?

MRS. LINDE: It's better that two people cling to the wreckage together rather than one person on his own.

KROGSTAD: Kristine.

MRS. LINDE: Why do you think I've come to this town?

KROGSTAD: Were you really thinking about me?

MRS. LINDE: If I'm to survive, I have to work. All my life, as long as I remember, I have worked. And there is no joy in working for yourself alone. Give me something, Nils. Give me someone to work for.

KROGSTAD: I don't believe this. This is a woman's hysterical, high-minded obsession with sacrificing herself —

MRS. LINDE: Have you ever known me to be hysterical?

KROGSTAD: Could you really do this? Could you? Tell me. Do you know all about my past life?

MRS. LINDE: Yes.

KROGSTAD: And you know my reputation here?

MRS. LINDE: You've just said, you've just implied, with me you could have been someone else.

KROGSTAD: I'm certain of it.

MRS. LINDE: Well then, surely it could still happen?

KROGSTAD: Kristine, do you know what you're saying?

MRS. LINDE: I need to care for someone, and your children need a mother. You and I need each other. Nils, I believe in you. I believe in what you really are. With you, I would have the courage to do anything. *(He clasps her hands.)*

KROGSTAD: Thank you — thank you — Kristine — I will make other people see me in the same way — but I forgot — *(She listens.)*

MRS. LINDE: Ssh. The dance upstairs, can you hear it? They'll be coming back when it's over.

KROGSTAD: You don't know what I've done to the Helmers, do you?

MRS. LINDE: I do know.

KROGSTAD: Even so, you've still the courage —

MRS. LINDE: I also know what a man like you can do in desperation.

KROGSTAD: If only I could stop what I've done

MRS. LINDE: You can. Your letter is still in the box.

KROGSTAD: Are you certain?

MRS. LINDE: Certain, but —

KROGSTAD: I will ask for my letter back.

MRS. LINDE: No, you will not.

KROGSTAD: I will, yes. I'll stay here till Helmer comes down.

MRS. LINDE: You must not ask for your letter back.

KROGSTAD: Wasn't that the reason you asked to meet me here?

MRS. LINDE: It was. I was frightened and didn't know better. They must be honest with each other.

KROGSTAD: Very well. If you want to take the responsibility — but one thing I can do and I will do it now — *(She listens.)*

MRS. LINDE: Hurry up. You must go. The dance is over. We have to leave now.

KROGSTAD: I'll wait for you downstairs.

MRS. LINDE: Do. You can walk me to my lodgings.

KROGSTAD: I am the happiest man in the whole wide world. *(He exits through the front door. The door between the room and the hall remains open.)*

MRS. LINDE: It's happened. *(She tidies up a little and gets her outdoor clothes.)* It's actually happened. Someone to work for, someone to live for. A home to bring joy to. I'll make it so comfortable. *(She listens, then puts on her hat and coat. Helmer and Nora's voices are heard in the hall. A key is turned and Helmer leads Nora into the hall, almost by force. She is dressed in the Italian costume, with a big, black shawl draped over her shoulders. He is wearing a dinner jacket with a big, black cloak. Still in the doorway, Nora resists him.)*

NORA: No, please, not yet, not in here, no. I want to go back upstairs. It's too early, I don't want to leave.

HELMER: My precious Nora, please —

NORA: I'm begging you, Torvald, I'm begging you please — one hour more, please.

HELMER: Not one minute more, my sweet Nora. We had an agreement, you know that. Now get into that drawing room or you will catch a chill. *(He leads her gently into the room, despite her resistance.)*

MRS. LINDE: Good evening.

NORA: Kristine?

HELMER: Mrs. Linde? Are you here so late? Why?

MRS. LINDE: Forgive me, yes. I so wanted to see Nora all dressed up.

NORA: You've been here waiting for me?

MRS. LINDE: I have. *(Helmer takes off Nora's shawl.)*

HELMER: Take a good look at her. She's worth looking at.

MRS. LINDE: Yes, I'd admit —

HELMER: Isn't she absolutely adorable? The entire party agreed. But she is a Miss Stubbornshoes. Imagine, I nearly had to drag her out of the room.

NORA: Torvald, you'll be sorry you didn't let me stay another half an hour.

HELMER: Do you hear her, Mrs. Linde? She dances her tarantella — she brings the house down — and she should have, she should have — though the performance was too much. Too reckless. I mean strictly speaking it went beyond the demands of art. Let that pass. She really did bring the house down. So should I have let her stay after that? Ruin the whole effect? Thank you, no. I took the arm of my lovely little girl from Capri — I should say my capricious little girl from Capri, and we moved through the room so swiftly, and as they say in novels, the beautiful vision was no more. An exit should really be an exit, Mrs. Linde, but I couldn't make Nora realize that. What's that noise? It's people leaving. Dear me, it's so hot in here. Please excuse me. *(He throws the cloak on a chair and opens the door to his study. He goes in and lights a few candles. Nora whispers quickly and breathlessly.)*

NORA: Well? *(Mrs. Linde answers quietly.)*

MRS. LINDE: I spoke to him.

NORA: And —

MRS. LINDE: Nora, tell your husband everything, you have to. *(Nora replies dully.)*

52

NORA: I knew.

MRS. LINDE: You have nothing to fear where Krogstad's concerned, but you must tell your husband. It's time you were honest.

NORA: I won't tell him.

MRS. LINDE: Then the letter will.

NORA: Thank you, Kristine. I know what needs to be done. *(Helmer returns.)*

HELMER: Now then, Mrs. Linde, have you had time to admire her.

MRS. LINDE: Yes. Now I must be leaving.

HELMER: So soon? Really? Is that your knitting?

MRS. LINDE: It is, thank you. I nearly forgot it. *(She takes it.)*

HELMER: So, you knit.

MRS. LINDE: I do.

HELMER: May I tell you something? Do embroidery instead.

MRS. LINDE: Why is that?

HELMER: Because it is much more attractive. You hold the embroidery in the left, and you move the needle with the right — like this — isn't that so?

MRS. LINDE: I suppose it is.

HELMER: But knitting — it's really quite ugly, isn't it? Look at me. Arms all squashed, knitting needles up and down — up and down — there is something Chinese about it. Excellent champagne tonight, they did themselves proud.

MRS. LINDE: Good night, Nora, and don't be stubborn any more.

HELMER: Hear hear, Mrs. Linde.

MRS. LINDE: Good night, Mr. Helmer. *(He accompanies her to the door.)*

HELMER: Good night, good night. You will get home safely, yes? I would be more than willing to go — but you don't have far to go. Good night, good night. *(She exits, he closes the door after her and returns.)* Dear God, we've got rid of her at last. That woman is extraordinarily boring.

NORA: Are you worn out, Torvald?

HELMER: I'm not — no, not at all.

NORA: Not sleepy even?

HELMER: I am not. I am wide awake. What about you? Yes, you do look a little sleepy.

NORA: I'm worn out, yes. I will sleep soon.

HELMER: Well, you see I was right not to let you stay any longer.

NORA: Everything you do is right. *(He kisses Nora's forehead.)*

HELMER: That's my little skylark. Did you see how cheerful Rank was this evening?

NORA: Was he? I didn't say a word to him.

HELMER: I said a few. But I've not seen him in such good form for a long time. *(He looks at her and moves a little closer.)* It's wonderful to be back at home. To be alone with you. Alone, together. I adore you, you beautiful girl.

NORA: Don't watch me like that, Torvald.

HELMER: You're my prize possession, why can't I watch you? Watch the lovely girl who is mine, mine entirely? You're mine. *(Nora goes to the other side of the table.)*

NORA: Don't speak to me like that tonight. *(He follows her.)*

HELMER: Your blood is still dancing the tarantella, I feel it. You are more and more desirable. Do you hear? The guests are starting to leave. Soon the whole house will be quiet. *(He lowers his voice.)*

NORA: I hope so.

HELMER: Yes, my beloved, my own Nora. Do you know, when I am at a party with you, do you know why I barely breathe a word to you, why I keep my distance? I'm pretending that you're my secret lover, that you're my young, secret fiancée — and no one knows there is anything between us.

NORA: Yes, I do, I do know. I know all your thoughts are about me.

HELMER: Then when we leave, and I take the shawl to wrap around your shoulders, around the wonderful curve of your neck, I imagine you're my bride so young, young, we have just been married, I'm taking you to my home, I am alone with you for the first time — alone together, you're trembling, beautiful, young. When I saw you sway and tempt me in the tarantella, my blood was on fire. I could not stand it. That's why I took you with me so early —

NORA: Go away Torvald. Leave me. I don't want this. Not tonight.

HELMER: What? Are you teasing me, Nora? Want — want. I'm your husband. *(A knock is heard on the front door. Nora starts. Helmer calls towards the hall.)* Who is that? *(Rank answers from outside.)*
RANK: It's me. Dare I come in? *(Helmer is quietly annoyed.)*
HELMER: One moment. *(He goes to open the door.)* How thoughtful of you not to pass by our door.
RANK: I thought I heard your voice, and I decided to look in. *(He glances around quickly.)* Yes, these loved, familiar rooms. It's so warm and cozy here with you.
HELMER: I thought you were very cozy upstairs as well.
RANK: Very much so. Why shouldn't I be? Why shouldn't one try everything in this life, yes? Try as much as you can, as long as you can. The wine was splendid.
HELMER: Especially the champagne.
RANK: You noticed that too? I can barely believe how much I managed to wash down.
NORA: Torvald drank his fair share of champagne tonight as well.
RANK: Did he?
NORA: Yes. And afterwards he is always in such a good mood.
RANK: Well, why shouldn't a man enjoy himself after a hard working day?
HELMER: Hard work? Sadly I can't claim that. *(Rank slaps Helmer's shoulders.)*
RANK: But I can, you see.
NORA: Dr. Rank, I think you carried out some scientific tests today.
RANK: Spot on. Yes.
HELMER: Little Nora speaking about scientific tests.
NORA: It went well?
RANK: The best possible result for both doctor and patient — certainty. *(Nora asks quickly and searchingly.)*
NORA: Certainty?
RANK: Absolute certainty. So shouldn't I allow myself a good evening after that?
HELMER: But don't end up suffering the morning after.
RANK: You get nothing for nothing in this life.
NORA: Dr. Rank, you do like fancy dress parties?
RANK: I do, as long as there are lots of exotic costumes —

NORA: Tell me, what shall we two next dress up as?

HELMER: You little silly — are you already thinking of the next ball?

RANK: We two? All right, I'll tell you, you shall be the Spirit of Joy —

HELMER: But what costume would convey that?

RANK: Your wife should appear in her everyday clothes —

HELMER: Well put. But what do you want to be?

RANK: My good friend, yes, I've no doubt about that.

HELMER: Well?

RANK: At the next fancy dress, I shall be invisible.

HELMER: What a strange thought.

RANK: There is a big black hat, and it makes you invisible. Didn't you know that story? You put it on and then no one can see you. *(Helmer suppresses a smile.)*

HELMER: Yes, you are right.

RANK: But I'm quite forgetting why I came. Helmer, give me a cigar, one of the black Havanas.

HELMER: With pleasure. *(He offers him the box. Rank takes one and cuts off the end.)*

RANK: Thank you. *(Nora strikes a match.)*

NORA: Let me light it.

RANK: Thank you. *(She holds up the match and he lights the cigar.)* And so — good-bye.

HELMER: Good-bye, old friend, good-bye.

NORA: Sleep well, Dr. Rank.

RANK: Thank you for your wish.

NORA: Wish me the same.

RANK: You? If you insist — sleep well. And thank you for the light. *(He nods to both and leaves. Helmer speaks quietly.)*

HELMER: He's downed a fair amount of drink. *(Nora answers absentmindedly.)*

NORA: He may have. *(Helmer takes out his keys and goes to the hall.)* Torvald, what are you doing?

HELMER: I have to empty the post box. It's nearly full. There won't be room for tomorrow's papers —

NORA: Do you want to work tonight?

HELMER: You know very well I don't. What's this? Someone's

been at the lock.

NORA: The lock?

HELMER: Yes. I wouldn't have thought the maids — here's a broken hair pin. It's one of yours, Nora — *(Nora answers quickly.)*

NORA: It must have been the children —

HELMER: You'll have to tell them never to do that. Anyway, I've managed to open it. *(He takes out the contents and shouts to the kitchen.)* Helene.

HELENE: Yes sir.

HELMER: Put out the lamp in the hall. Good night.

HELENE: Good night, sir. *(He enters the living room and closes the door to the hall. He stands with the letters in his hand.)*

HELMER: Do you see how they've piled up? *(He leafs through the pile.)* What is this? *(Nora is by the window.)*

NORA: The letter. No, Torvald, no.

HELMER: Two visiting cards from Rank.

NORA: Do they say anything?

HELMER: A black cross above his name — look. What an appalling idea. It's as if he's announcing his own death.

NORA: He is.

HELMER: Do you know something? Has he told you something?

NORA: When the cards come, he is saying good-bye to us. He wants to go and die by himself.

HELMER: My poor friend.

NORA: I didn't think it would be so soon. *(Torvald paces the room.)*

HELMER: Perhaps, it is for the best like this. For him at any rate. *(He stops.)* For us too, perhaps, Nora. Now we've only got each other. *(Helmer throws his arms around Nora.)* Darling, how can I hold you tightly enough? Nora, do you know that I've often wished you were facing some terrible dangers that I could risk life and limb, risk everything for your sake? *(Nora tears herself away and speaks in a strong, determined voice.)*

NORA: Read your letters. Now, Torvald.

HELMER: Not tonight. No. I want to be with you, my darling wife.

NORA: Your friend's dying — think of him —

HELMER: Yes, you're right. This has upset the two of us. This ugly thing has come between us. Death and decay. We should clear our minds of that. Until then, we will go to our own rooms. *(Nora is around his neck.)*

NORA: Torvald, good night. *(Helmer kisses her on the forehead.)*

HELMER: Good night, my little singing bird. Sleep well, Nora. I'm going to read all these letters from beginning to end. *(He goes with the bundle in his hand into his study and closes the door behind him. With despair in her eyes, Nora fumbles about, gets hold of Helmer's cloak, throws it about herself, whispering quickly, brokenly, hoarsely.)*

NORA: I will never see him again. Never. Never. Never. *(She throws her shawl over her head.)* Children, never see them again. Not them either. Never. The black, cold, icy water. Down and down, without end — if it would only end. Now he's got it. Now he's reading it. No. Not yet. Torvald, good-bye and, children — *(She is about to rush through the hall. At the same time Helmer throws open his door and stands with an opened letter in his hand.)*

HELMER: Nora. *(She screams loudly.)* What is this? Do you know what's written in this letter?

NORA: I know. Let me go. Let me leave. *(He holds her back.)*

HELMER: Where are you going?

NORA: Torvald, don't save me. *(He staggers back.)*

HELMER: Is what he writes true? It's horrible. It can't possibly be true.

NORA: It's all true. I've loved you more than anything else in this whole world —

HELMER: Don't give me your pathetic excuses. *(She takes a step towards him.)*

NORA: Torvald —

HELMER: You pathetic fool, do you know what you've done?

NORA: Let me leave. You're not going to suffer for my sake. You're not going to take the blame.

HELMER: Stop playacting. *(He locks the door.)* You will explain here and now. Do you understand what you've done? Answer me. Do you understand what you've done? *(Nora looks at him steadily and answers with a frozen expression.)*

NORA: Yes. Now I'm beginning to understand. *(Helmer paces the floor.)*

HELMER: I've really had my eyes opened. In all these years. You who were my pride and joy, a hypocrite! A liar! Worse! A criminal!

The ugliness of it all. *(Nora is silent. She stares at him without blinking. Helmer stops in front of her.)* I should have known something like this would happen. Your father was a reckless man, and you are his reckless daughter — don't interrupt. No religion, no morals, no sense of duty. I'm being punished for closing my eyes to his faults. I did it for your sake. This is how you repay me.

NORA: Yes, this is how.

HELMER: Now you've wrecked my happiness. You've thrown away my whole future. I am at the mercy of a man with no conscience. He can do as he likes with me, demand what he wants from me, he can bully and command me as he pleases. I daren't complain. I will have to sink, I'm going under because of you, woman.

NORA: When I'm out of the way, you'll be free.

HELMER: Spare me your dramatic gestures. Your father was always ready with that kind of talk. You, out of the way? How in the hell would that help me? He can let this whole business be known anyway. People might think that I was behind it — that I encouraged you. And it's you I can thank for all of this. You that I carried with my two hands throughout our entire marriage. Do you understand what you've done to me? *(Nora is calmly cold.)*

NORA: I do.

HELMER: That's what is so unbelievable. That I can't take in. Still we must deal with it. Take off your shawl. Take it off, I say. I must try to satisfy him in some way. This has to be kept quiet at any price. And as far as we're concerned, we must look as if nothing has changed. But only in public. From now on you will stay in the house. But you won't be allowed to bring up the children. I daren't trust you with them. To have to say this to the woman I loved and still — But that's behind us now — in the past. From now on, forget happiness. Now it's just about saving the remains, the wreckage, the appearance. *(The front door bell rings. Helmer starts.)* What is it? It's late. Nora, hide, say you're sick! *(She stands without moving as Helmer goes to open the door to the hall. The Maid, half dressed, appears in the doorway.)*

MAID: A letter. Addressed to you, Mrs. Helmer.

HELMER: Give me it. *(He grasps the letter and closes the door.)* It's from him, yes. You won't get it. I'll read it myself.

NORA: You read it. *(Helmer is by the lamp.)*

HELMER: We may be ruined, you and me. *(He tears open the letter in a hurry, reads it, looks at an enclosed paper and gives a cry of joy.)* Nora. *(Nora looks at him inquisitively.)* Nora. I must read it again. Yes. Yes. It's true. I'm saved. Nora, I'm saved. I am.

NORA: And me?

HELMER: You too, naturally. We're both saved, you and me. Look. Your contract, he's returning it. He regrets, he repents, he says. His life has taken a turn for the better — who cares what he says? Nora, we're saved. No one can harm you. Nora. Nora, let's get rid of this hideous thing. *(He glances at the paper.)* I won't look at it. A bad dream, that's all it's been. *(He tears the contract, both letters into pieces. He throws every thing into the stove, and watches it burn.)* There. They don't exist any more. He says that since Christmas Eve, you — they must have been three dreadful days for you, Nora.

NORA: I fought a hard battle these past three days.

HELMER: And you tortured yourself, you could see no way out but to — No, we won't remember ugliness. We'll be happy and we'll keep saying, it's finished, it's finished. Listen to me, Nora, you don't seem to understand. It's finished. Now what's this — this cold expression? Dear little Nora, I do know. You just can't believe that I've forgiven you everything. I do know that what you did you did out of love for me.

NORA: Yes, I did.

HELMER: A wife should love her husband, and that's how you love me. But the ends didn't justify the means in this case, and you didn't have the knowledge to realize that. Do you think I love you less because you don't know how to act on your own? No. Lean on me. I'll advise you. I'll teach you. I wouldn't be much of a man if your being helpless didn't make you doubly attractive. Don't pay any heed to my harsh words earlier. I was frightened then. I thought everything would collapse on top of me. I've forgiven you, Nora. I swear to you I've forgiven you.

NORA: Thank you for your forgiveness. *(She exits through the door stage R.)*

HELMER: Don't go — *(He looks in.)* What are you up to, in your room? *(Nora speaks offstage.)*

NORA: Taking off my fancy dress. *(He is by the open door.)*

HELMER: Do, that, yes. Then calm down and collect your thoughts, my frightened singing bird. You can rest now. I have big wings to cover you. *(He paces close to the door.)* Our home is so cozy, so lovely, Nora. There's shelter for you here. I'll watch over you. I've saved you from the hawk's claws, and they've hunted you, you poor dove. Your heart's beating, I'll calm it. It will happen bit by bit. Nora, believe me — tomorrow everything will look quite different to you. Everything will soon be like it was before. I'll have no need to tell you I forgive you. You'll feel yourself that it's certain I have. How could you even think I could dismiss you and even blame you for anything? You don't know what a real heart — a man's heart is, Nora. How can I describe it? There is something so sweet, so satisfying for a man to know in himself that he has forgiven his wife. He's forgiven her from the bottom of his heart. It's as if he's twice made her his own. It's like he's given her a new life. In a way she has become his wife and his child. From now on that's what you'll be for me. You bewildered, helpless, little creature. Nora, don't be frightened of anything, whatever you need tell me. I will be your strength and your conscience. What's this? I thought you had gone to bed. Have you changed? *(Nora is in her day clothes.)*

NORA: Yes, Torvald, I've changed now.

HELMER: But it's so late why?

NORA: I won't sleep tonight.

HELMER: But Nora, my dear — *(She looks at her watch.)*

NORA: It's not very late yet. Torvald, sit down. We have to talk to each other. *(She sits down on one side of the table.)*

HELMER: What is this, Nora? You're looking so coldly at me —

NORA: Sit down. I have to talk to you. *(He sits at the other side of the table.)*

HELMER: You worry me, Nora. I don't understand you.

NORA: No. That's just it. You do not understand me. I have never understood you either. Until tonight. Do not interrupt me. Listen to me. Torvald, it is time to be honest.

HELMER: What do you mean? *(There is a short pause.)*

NORA: Does anything strike you about the way we're sitting here?

HELMER: What?

NORA: We've been married now for eight years. This is the first time the two of us, man and wife are having a serious conversation.

HELMER: What do you mean serious?

NORA: For eight whole years — longer even — from the first day we met, we have never sat down and exchanged one serious word about serious things.

HELMER: So I should have shared worries that you could never have helped me with anyway?

NORA: I'm not talking about worries. I'm saying that we have never sat down and seriously tried to get to the heart of anything.

HELMER: But Nora what good would that have been to you?

NORA: That's the point. You've never understood me. I've been wronged, Torvald, and badly so. First by Papa, and then by you.

HELMER: What? Us? The two who have loved you more than anyone else? *(Nora shakes her head.)*

NORA: You never loved me. You just thought it was fun to be in love with me.

HELMER: What are you saying, Nora?

NORA: The truth, Torvald. When I lived with Papa he told me his opinions about everything, and I had the same opinions. If I thought differently, I hid it. Because he wouldn't have liked it. He called me his little doll, and he played with me the same way I played with my dolls. Then I came to your house —

HELMER: What kind of expression is that? This is our marriage you're talking about. *(She is undisturbed.)*

NORA: I was handed from Papa to you. You organized everything according to your taste, and I picked up the same taste as you. Or I just pretended to. I don't really know. I think I did both. First one, then the other. When I look back at it now, it seems to me that I have been living like a beggar, from hand to mouth. I have been performing tricks for you, Torvald. That's how I've survived. You wanted it like that. You and Papa have done me a great harm. It's because of you I've made nothing of myself.

HELMER: That's not rational, Nora, and it's not grateful. Have you not been happy here in this house?

NORA: No, I have never been happy here. I thought I was, but I never was.

HELMER: Not happy? Never —

NORA: No. Just cheerful. And you were always kind to me. But our home was just a playroom. Here, where I've been your doll-wife, the way I was Papa's doll-child. The children, they became my dolls. I thought it was fun when you played with me Torvald, the same way they thought it fun when I played with them. Our marriage, Torvald, that is what it's been.

HELMER: There is some truth in what you say, even if it is exaggerated and hysterical. But that time is over now. Playtime is over. It's time for teaching.

NORA: Who will be taught? Me or the children?

HELMER: Both you and the children, Nora my love.

NORA: Torvald, you are not the man to teach me how to be the proper wife for you.

HELMER: How can you say that?

NORA: And me — how am I equipped to teach the children?

HELMER: Nora.

NORA: Didn't you say that to me just now? You didn't dare trust me with them.

HELMER: In a moment of anger. Why take any notice of that?

NORA: Because what you said was true. I'm not equipped for it. I must do something else first. I must educate myself. You are not the man to help me with that. I have to do it on my own. That's why I'm leaving you now. *(He jumps up.)*

HELMER: What did you say?

NORA: I must stand on my own if I'm to make sense of myself and everything around me. That's why I can't live with you any longer.

HELMER: Nora, Nora.

NORA: I'll leave now. Kristine will put me up for tonight.

HELMER: You are mad. I won't allow you. I forbid you.

NORA: It's no use forbidding me anything any more. I'll take what is mine with me. I want nothing from you now or ever again.

HELMER: What kind of lunacy is this?

NORA: I'm going home tomorrow, to my old home, I mean. It will be easier for me to find something to do there.

HELMER: You can't see what you're doing, you have no experience.

NORA: Then I must get experience, Torvald.

HELMER: Abandon your home, abandon your husband, abandon your children? What do you think people will say?

NORA: I can't take any notice of that. I just know what I must do.

HELMER: This is monstrous. Can you abandon your most sacred duties like this?

NORA: What do you think my most sacred duties are?

HELMER: Do I need to tell you that? You have a duty to your husband and your children, don't you?

NORA: I have other duties that are just as sacred.

HELMER: No, you haven't. Tell me them.

NORA: My duties to myself.

HELMER: You are a wife and a mother before everything else.

NORA: I don't believe that any more. I believe that I am a human being, just as much as you are — or at least I will try to become one. I know most people would agree with you, Torvald. And books say things like that. I can't listen to that any more. I can't live like that any more. I just can't. I have to find out these things for myself and find out about them.

HELMER: Don't you understand your place in your own home? Don't you have an infallible guide? Haven't you got religion?

NORA: Torvald, I don't even know what religion is.

HELMER: What are you saying?

NORA: I only know what Pastor Hansen told me when I was confirmed. He said religion meant this and that. When I am away from all of this, when I'm own my own, I'll think over this too. I want to see if what Pastor Hansen told me was right, or at least if it's right for me.

HELMER: This is unheard of coming from a young woman. But if you reject religion, what about your conscience? Are you still in touch with any morality? Or maybe you have none. Answer me.

NORA: It's not easy to answer that, Torvald. I don't know really. I'm very confused about those things. But I do know I think differently from you. I now find out the law differs from what I'd imagined. I simply can't believe that the law should be right. A woman is not allowed to spare her old, dying father, or to save her husband's life — I don't believe that.

HELMER: You're speaking like a child. You don't understand

64

the society you live in.

NORA: I don't, no. But now I'm about to find out. I must find out who's right — society or me.

HELMER: You're ill, Nora. You're feverish. I almost think you've taken leave of your senses.

NORA: I've never felt so clear and certain, as tonight.

HELMER: So clear and certain that you abandon your husband and abandon your children?

NORA: I do, yes.

HELMER: There's only one way to explain this.

NORA: What?

HELMER: You don't love me any more.

NORA: No, I don't.

HELMER: Nora, how can you say that?

NORA: It hurts me very much, Torvald, because you have always been so generous to me. But I can't help it. I do not love you any more. *(Helmer forces his self-control.)*

HELMER: And are you clear and certain on that too?

NORA: Yes, absolutely clear, absolutely certain. That's why I don't want to stay here any more.

HELMER: Can you tell me how I lost your love?

NORA: Yes, I can. It was tonight, when something glorious didn't happen, because then I saw you were not the man I thought you were.

HELMER: Explain yourself. I don't understand you.

NORA: I've been patiently waiting for eight years, because God knows I do realize that glorious things don't happen every day. Then this dreadful blow hit me, and I was utterly certain that now something glorious would happen. When Krogstad's letter lay out there, I never thought you would accept that man's conditions. I was so utterly certain of what you would say to him. Tell the truth to the whole world. And when that happened —

HELMER: What then? When I'd exposed my wife to shame and humiliation —

NORA: When that had happened, I believed with absolute certainty that you would step forward, you would take the blame, you would say, "I am the guilty one."

HELMER: Nora —

NORA: You believe I would never have allowed such a huge sacrifice from you. No, of course not. But what would what I have to say count against what you had to say. That was the glorious thing I hoped for and feared. And to stop that happening, I was prepared to give my life.

HELMER: Nora, for you I would have worked day and night. For your sake I would have suffered any sorrow or hardship. But no man sacrifices his integrity for the person he loves.

NORA: Hundreds of thousands of women have.

HELMER: You're thinking and speaking like an ignorant child.

NORA: Be that as it may, but you don't think, or speak like a man I can share my life with. When you stopped being frightened, it was not of what was threatening me: you were frightened of what you had to face. When you stopped being frightened, it was as if nothing had happened. I was your little singing bird just like before. Your doll, that you would carry now with twice the care, since it was so weak and fragile. *(She gets up.)* Torvald, at that moment, I realized I'd spent the last eight years of my life married to a total stranger and that I'd borne him three children ... I can't bear to think of it. It tears me to pieces. *(Helmer speaks sadly.)*

HELMER: I see now. I see. There's an abyss between us. Yes. Nora, can we not reach across it?

NORA: The way I am now, I am no wife to you.

HELMER: I have the strength to be another man.

NORA: Perhaps — if your doll is taken from you.

HELMER: Separated — separated from you? No, Nora, I can't bear that thought. *(She goes to the room stage R.)*

NORA: That makes it all the more necessary that it has to happen. It has to. *(She returns with her coat and a small bag which she puts on the chair by the table.)*

HELMER: Nora, not now. Wait till tomorrow, Nora. *(She puts on her coat.)*

NORA: I can't spend the night in a stranger's house.

HELMER: Can we not live here as brother and sister —

NORA: You know very well that wouldn't last long. *(She wraps the shawl around herself.)* Good-bye, Torvald. I don't want to see the children. They're in better hands than mine, I'm sure. I can be of no use to them, the way I am now.

HELMER: But some day, Nora, some day —

NORA: How do I know? I don't even know what will happen to me.

HELMER: But you're my wife, you are now, you always will be my wife.

NORA: Listen, Torvald, when a wife walks out of her husband's house, as I'm walking out now, to the best of my knowledge the law frees him completely from her. In any case, I'm freeing you completely. Don't feel you're tied in any way, no more than I will be. We both must be completely free. Look, here's your ring. Give me mine.

HELMER: That as well?

NORA: That as well.

HELMER: Here it is.

NORA: Yes, now it is finished. I will put my keys here. The maids know everything about the house — better than I do. Tomorrow, when I've gone, Kristine will come here and pack the things that I brought from home. I will have them sent on to me.

HELMER: Finished, finished. Will you ever think of me, Nora?

NORA: I'll think of you often and of the children and the house here.

HELMER: Nora, can I write to you?

NORA: No — never. I won't allow you that.

HELMER: At least can I send you —

NORA: Nothing. Nothing.

HELMER: Let me help you, if you need it.

NORA: No. I'm telling you I take nothing from strangers.

HELMER: Can I never be anything but a stranger to you, Nora? *(Nora takes her bag.)*

NORA: Torvald, then something really glorious would have to happen —

HELMER: What is this glorious thing?

NORA: You and I would both have to change so much that — Torvald, I don't believe in glorious things any more.

HELMER: But I want to believe in them. Say it. Change so much that — ?

NORA: That our marriage could become a life together. Good-bye. *(She exits through the hall. He sinks down in a chair by the door*

and buries his face in his hands.)
HELMER: Nora, Nora. *(He looks around and gets up.)* Empty. She is not here any more. *(A hope rises in him.)* Something glorious —
(Downstairs the street door slams shut.)

PROPERTY LIST

Packages with Christmas gifts (NORA)
Christmas tree (MESSENGER)
Basket (MESSENGER)
Purse with money (NORA)
Bag of macaroons (NORA)
Pen (HELMER)
Wallet with money (bills) (HELMER)
Piece of paper (KROGSTAD)
Box with costume pieces (NANNY)
Bundle of papers (HELMER)
Lamp (MAID)
Visiting card (MAID)
Book (MRS. LINDE)
Watch (MRS. LINDE)
Knitting paraphernalia (MRS. LINDE)
Box of cigars (HELMER)
Match (NORA)
Keys (HELMER)
Bundle of letters (HELMER)
Visiting cards (HELMER)
Opened letter and contract (HELMER)
Letter (MAID)
Watch (NORA)
Small bag (NORA)

SOUND EFFECTS

Door bell
Footsteps
Door slam

NOTES
(Use this space to make notes for your production)

NOTES

(Use this space to make notes for your production)